PRAISE FOR

THE ART OF GETTING IT WRONG

Open-hearted vulnerability. A real pleasure to read and a reminder of the best in all of us. I was encouraged and inspired. Thanks, Stephen!

Leslie Odom Jr., two-time Academy Award nominee as *Hamilton*'s Aaron Burr, and author of *Failing Up*

In his closing remarks in this book, Stephen Miller observes that "the world tends to write our victories in the sand while etching our failures in concrete." In our more honest moments, most of us must also admit that we do this very thing to ourselves. The negative verdicts that occupy our minds and hearts throughout the day about never measuring up, about being too much of "this" or not enough of "that," can form us in such a way that the gremlins of regret, shame, and failure become our heart mentors. That's what makes books like *The Art of Getting it Wrong*, and transparent and serious writers like Stephen, so needed and helpful. Stephen effectively points us back to the reality that what is true for him is also true for us. It's all going to be okay, because God cannot stop loving us and has secured the greatest future for us.

Scott Sauls, senior pastor, Christ Presbyterian Church, Nashville, Tennessee, and author of *Beautiful People Don't Just Happen*

As someone who has lots of experience "getting it wrong," this book provided encouragement and instruction on how to let our mishaps *refine* us instead of *define* us. Written in Stephen Miller's classic humor, we found ourselves delightfully challenged from start to finish.

Andrew East and Shawn Johnson East, former National Football League player and Olympic gold gymnast/The East Fam

With his trademark passion, humor, and optimism, Stephen Miller brings an important and timely message for us in *The Art of Getting It Wrong*. We all need a friend who can remind us that it's going to be okay, even when life's disappointments, failures, or deep hurts threaten to pull us down. It may not feel like it now, but it's going to be okay. Personally, I need this perspective more than ever. If you find yourself in this place too, you'll want to read this book!

Lysa TerKeurst, #1 *New York Times* bestselling
author and president of Proverbs 31

We're so encouraged by Stephen's unabashed self-reflection and message that we aren't bound or defined by our failures. Our God is orchestrating a powerful story in us all. We all struggle with self-doubt and fear in the hard moments in life, and this book is like a warm hug!

Adam and Danielle Busby, *OutDaughtered* on TLC and
It's A Buzz World YouTube channel

Through his faith, relatable movie quotes, and self-deprecating humor, Stephen Miller takes us on a journey through his life and shows us that we are not the sums of our mistakes; we are what we *learn* from them. *The Art of Getting It Wrong* is exactly the type of message this world needs today—a message that no matter how bad we may feel about failure, we are simply going to be okay. Excellent read!

Shaun and Mindy McKnight, Cute Girls Hairstyles

In *The Art of Getting It Wrong*, Stephen Miller reminds us that we do not need to be defined by our worst moments. If you find yourself trying to get back up after falling down, you'll find this book brimming with encouragement and buoyant with hope.

Dr. Darren Whitehead, lead pastor, Church of
the City, Nashville, Tennessee

THE ART OF
GETTING IT WRONG

THE ART OF GETTING IT WRONG

FINDING GOOD IN THE MISADVENTURES OF LIFE

STEPHEN MILLER

ZONDERVAN BOOKS

ZONDERVAN BOOKS

The Art of Getting It Wrong
Copyright © 2022 by Stephen Miller

Requests for information should be addressed to:
Zondervan, *3900 Sparks Dr. SE, Grand Rapids, Michigan 49546*

Zondervan titles may be purchased in bulk for educational, business, fundraising, or sales promotional use. For information, please email SpecialMarkets@Zondervan.com.

ISBN 978-0-310-36469-6 (hardcover)
ISBN 978-0-310-36472-6 (audio)
ISBN 978-0-310-36471-9 (ebook)

The author is represented by Tom Dean, literary agent with A Drop of Ink LLC, www.adropofink.pub.

Cover design: Curt Diepenhorst
Cover photo: Micah Kandros
Interior design: Sara Colley

Printed in the United States of America

22 23 24 25 26 27 28 29 30 /LSC/ 12 11 10 9 8 7 6 5 4 3 2 1

Dedicated to Amanda, Reese, Penny, Keira,
Jude, Liam, Ethan, and Lincoln—
you are the light of my life,
my greatest honor and joy.
I love you all with everything I am.

In loving memory of Jim Frith and Darrin Patrick—
two men who taught me more about life, manhood, and Jesus
than probably anyone else on earth.
Miss you both dearly.
Can't wait to party with you one day!

CONTENTS

FOREWORD

I don't think it surprises anyone to say that YouTube can be a pretty pretentious place. Like it's hard to know what's real and what's not. A lot of people get caught up in the drama and clickbait to get the views. And that can make people cynical, which sucks. So Savannah and I always notice when we find a family that's actually real . . . who are marked by just honest, authentic love. We ourselves, through our own family, have really tried to show this kind of authentic love that inspires people. We've shared a lot of ups and downs, highs and lows, and somehow by God's grace, we've had more than 13 million people decide to join us as subscribers, which is honestly pretty mind-blowing. That's why we love The Miller Fam and Stephen! That's who Stephen is! Just a dude being real—mistakes and all (like a lot of them)—and inviting people into his journey. He and Amanda have created a space that shows the beauty and the brokenness of marriage, adoption, parenting with special needs, and having a gigantic family.

Stephen is a lot like me in so many ways—a goofy, go-big-or-go-home kind of guy with dreams to change the world. He loves Jesus and loves his wife and loves his kids, and the wisdom he has written in this book is something I really hope everyone reads. It's something I wish I would have been able to read years ago! We all get it wrong sometimes.

Some of us more than others. But the truth stays the same, whether we screw up all the time or only every once in a while.

The thing I love about Stephen is his transparency about his failures. How he learns from them, and then shares them with us so we can learn too! He doesn't shy away from showing us the embarrassing parts that will make us cringe and groan and look inward and say, *Oh, that's kinda me too.* He's like that dad who somehow knows just the perfect way to get the point across so everyone gets it, and he's not preachy or judgy or holier-than-thou. He's just real and hilarious.

This book you're about to read contains some of the most insanely funny, true stories of getting it wrong, maybe ever. Like I laughed from cover to cover. But I'm pretty sure that after you read them, you won't think less of Stephen as much as think that if God can do something cool with him, he's not done with you yet either. God knows all you've done and all you will do and loves you anyway—mistakes and all. I'm so excited that you picked up this book. I hope you read it from cover to cover, take notes, underline, share it on social media, and are really encouraged by it. I know that's what Stephen wants too!

COLE LABRANT, The LaBrant Fam

CHAPTER 1

WHAT'S UP, BEAUTIFUL PEOPLE?

W hat's up, beautiful people?" I've said these words what seems like a million times.

If you're unfamiliar with us, my family and I create videos chronicling our journey as a gigantic, diverse family of nine, and while I'm not quite sure how we started it, we open every video with those four words. They're a simple, subtle reminder that you—yes, you—have more value and worth than you could ever possibly imagine. You matter.

And as easily as these words roll off my tongue—a sort of slogan—if I'm being honest, I don't always feel like the slogan applies to me. I feel a bit of an imposter. I'm *supposed* to be the guy who has it all together. The guy who loves his wife and his kids perfectly every day, no hiccups, mess-ups, do-overs, or slips of the tongue that put me in the proverbial doghouse (and as you'll see, I've had a few doozies in my day that definitely would have had me sleeping with the dogs if we had any).

But we all know that's not completely true all the time, right? Like, that is an inherently impossible ideal for *anyone* to aspire to!

Sometimes my kids are being crazy or Amanda and I just got in an argument or I just feel ugly and fat and like my hair looks like a crapola sundae with a poo cherry on top and I have literally no desire whatsoever to try to film a video. I feel like a fake, phony caricature who is the furthest thing from "beautiful people."

And yet I know from personal experience that even if I don't always feel it, saying something so subtly and simply profound has a way of pulling me out of the funk. There is power in reminding ourselves of what's true in the face of feelings that don't always line up with the facts.

That's the baseline for everything I'm gonna write in this book. It's the jumping-off point for all the craziness I'm gonna attempt to say. And believe me, I can say some crazy stuff.

At the heart of it all, I'm a dad. I joke that I'm a father of many nations, though in reality it's only three nations, which I would normally call *a few* but some books count as *many*, so I'm going with it. For the last eighteen years, I've raised seven little balls of cuteness and crazy. That's basically half of my lifetime thus far, so I can't help but see the world through the lens of a dad. It's the father's heart in me that wants so desperately for you to know that you are seen. You belong. You are loved. No matter what is making you anxious about tomorrow or how many times you may have failed, even just today, it's gonna be okay.

> There is power in reminding ourselves of what's true.

TV DAD

Growing up, I would watch family sitcom after family sitcom. As a general rule, the dad was a super-goofy guy who without fail had some giant gaffe that needed fixing, but the amazing thing was that no matter how idiotic he may have come across as, he was consistent. He loved his kids. And as silly as he was, he was still full of the wisdom he had amassed from all the failures and flops along the way, and he was more than willing and able to pass on that wisdom to them.

The sitcom dad is the only dad a lot of kids grew up with. *TGIF* was like a church for a whole generation looking for peace from the Friday-night-silver-screen light. There was something soothing about it. Something comforting. Something that gave a feeling of security our hearts were longing for. At the end of the day, no matter how crazy it got, we had the sense it was gonna be okay. Even if that moment of escape into the sitcom reality was the only thing in our lives that was okay that day, it was a moment of comfort that we needed.

I'm a lot more like the slapstick sitcom dad than I want to admit sometimes. I trip over myself because I've got both feet securely stuffed in my mouth. I break stuff and forget everything and make a fool of myself all the time. I lose my keys just about every day and find them in the most random places.

Even this morning, I found myself stranded at the gym because I couldn't remember where I had left my keys. I was convinced I had left them in a particular locker, but there was a padlock on it. I thought I was going crazy and was determined to prove myself wrong. But after meticulously searching the gym floor and every other unlocked locker in the room, I was pretty sure someone had conveniently placed *their* stuff in *my* locker and proceeded to put a padlock on it, thus preventing me from leaving. I was so certain it was *my* locker that I got bolt cutters and cut their padlock off, posting a note that read, "You locked my keys in your locker (*implied: you idiot!*), so I cut off your padlock and got them. Sorry for the inconvenience." My wife tells me I am passive-aggressive sometimes. I have no clue what she means.

I had it all worked out. I executed the plan with the kind of adept proficiency you might see in a *Mission: Impossible* episode or *Ocean's Eleven* movie. It was like a work of art. And I was fully prepared to bask in the glory of seeing a plan come together. I even briefly considered buying a celebratory cigar and calling up Mr. T for a high five afterward.

Only one problem. I don't actually know Mr. T. Also, my keys were not in "my" locker. I guess that's two problems.

Feeling incredibly sheepish and unwilling to make a fool of myself yet again by going on a mad padlock-cutting spree, I sat there quietly

THE ART OF GETTING IT WRONG

in the locker room like a sniper waiting for the right shot as every single person came through to collect their belongings.

After an hour of looking like a crazy, lazy locker stalker, two men walked in and opened the lockers *next* to the one I *thought* I had put my stuff in. I could feel the sensation of hope mingled with utter disdain rising up in my soul as the man retrieved his bag and immediately gasped, "Oh my gosh!"

His eyes were as big as dinner plates.

I sprung up with a quick, halfway-laughing "I'll take them," grabbed my keys, and left as rapidly as my embarrassed, frustrated feet could carry me out of the gym. Someone had locked my keys in their locker. But I cut the wrong lock and now some poor, unassuming businessman with the nicest khakis I'd ever seen needs a new padlock.

During my search, I was calculating every single possible scenario of what could have happened.

Did someone steal my van? That gloriously large bus that carts my ginormous family around? I need that thing! Will insurance cover it or will they leave me holding the bill because I failed to lock my locker, inviting some van-loving hoodlum to commandeer my hard-earned party wagon? We had carefully chosen that specific van because of its mullet-like nature of business in the front, party in the back. It got the job done of moving our little army from place to place without giving off the vibe that we might be trying to steal your kid for some devious purpose other than taking them to soccer practice. And now I might not have it anymore!

How will I get home? Am I gonna be out like $150 to get a new key made? What will my wife say when I tell her I lost my keys? Will she believe me that I didn't just misplace them yet again? Likely story! How will I cope with the shame of that? Everyone is gonna make fun of me. The people at the front desk think I'm crazy.

Every thought imaginable. All the panic and anxiety and anger and fear and frustration assaulting me at the same time.

And just as quickly as the onslaught of worry whisked me away, the three words of "Oh my gosh" chased them back into the shadows. My fears were unfounded. It was gonna be okay.

And honestly, regardless of the outcome, even if my worst fears had been realized, it would have still been okay.

Even our worst fears and failures can somehow become our greatest blessings.

These little events keep reminding me of that. They give me perspective.

Kinda like Bob Ross. I feel like Bob Ross had quite literally mastered the *art* of getting it wrong. This dude somehow found a way to turn even the biggest mess-up into some happy little trees with fluffy little clouds, and then if he missed any other happy little accidents, well, let's just make them birds. Yeah, they're birds now.

I have a ton of lessons I learned from that little frustrating failure in the locker room. I'm hoping I can pull out some TV dad wisdom for all of us. Maybe the first lesson is this: be quick with the patience and slow with the bolt cutters.

Perhaps I'll buy that khakis-wearing businessman the best padlock Target has to offer. And while I'm at it, I should probably get one for myself too.

WE ARE ALL BECOMING SOMETHING

At the end of the day, the most common job I have as a dad is not being perfect or omnipotent. It's not being able to fix broken stuff or be good at math or get everything on the list at the grocery store. It's not (*not*) losing my keys in the weirdest ways possible.

It's holding my kids in my arms and, as reassuringly as I know how, drawing from the well of year after year of finding this one truth to be consistently and constantly true: it's gonna be okay.

No matter how old they are. No matter the situation. No matter how big their mess-up or mistake. No matter how badly they got it wrong. No matter whether it's one of my daughters or one of my sons. It's gonna be okay.

And that's really what this book is. Just a dad trying his best to take you guys in and tell you, "Hey, beautiful people, it's gonna be okay."

As the world's leading expert on what it means to mess up royally,[1] I understand that we get one shot at this life. There are no substitutions, exchanges, or refunds on our experiences.

We are all picking up this book with our own experiences of trauma and consequences and heartbreak from decisions we have made.

We are all walking through the pain of decisions that have been made about us and deciding how to react to those moments in ways that hopefully give us life. Sometimes we do that in ways that are healthy and helpful. Sometimes not so much.

And that's okay. That's part of being human. As a dad, my job is not to try to invalidate your feelings or tell you that no matter what, it's all gonna be rainbows and butterflies. First off, you may be in the minority of people who hate rainbows. Or perhaps you're allergic to butterflies. I'm not here to make light of your situations or in any way insinuate that they're not as bad as they are. You are free to feel every feeling as deeply as you can and you are free to let healing overwhelm you and carry you to new heights.

That's what you're here for.

I'm simply here to offer some experience that will hopefully tilt your perspective to see that in and through it all, somehow, it's being used to shape you into someone who is better than you were before.

Your perspective has more power than your circumstances have—how you see yourself, the world, the people around you. In every situation you get to decide to be a victor rather than a victim. To recognize this is not happening *to* you but happening *for* you. Whether it's for you personally, or to one day help someone else.

You can get more out of your mess-ups than you lost from them.

Your failures can feed your fears or seed your blessings. The choice is up to you.

As for me, I'm trying to be a lot less like Chicken Little, always screaming, "THE SKY IS FALLING!" and be a lot more like Louis Prima, singing, "If every time it rains, it rains, pennies from heaven!"[2] And we can't forget the Shooby Dooby. That's key. I wanna be a Shooby-Dooby kinda guy who sees the storms and suckiness and silliness as though it were happening for my good—making me, molding me, maturing me, moving me.

> Your perspective has more power than your circumstances have.

We are all moving somewhere, becoming something. Forward or backward. Up or down. Left or right. We rarely have the option of staying stagnant. That's not how life works. And wouldn't it be boring if it did? I think we would soon be like pond scum, stinking and swarming with mosquitos. But we aren't pond scum. We're beautiful people. On a beautiful journey, mistakes and all. And at the end of this journey, it really is gonna be okay. So let's freaking go!

CHAPTER 2

THE ART OF THE EPIC FAIL

A t the risk of sounding like I'm in a twelve-step self-help program . . .
Hi, my name is Stephen, and I'm a failure.

Like, an epic failure. I know the word *epic* is probably so hackneyed at this point that maybe you rolled your eyes, but the actual meaning of the word denotes a ridiculously long story that's so outlandish it's a little hard to believe.

Yep, that sounds about right.

People often quote Mark Twain for having once famously said, "The report of my death has been greatly exaggerated."[3] Whether he said these exact words or the quote itself has been exaggerated in true Mark Twain style over time, this may be his most hilarious, tweet-worthy "quote" ever because, as you know, you can't quite exaggerate a scientific, physiological fact like that—even for Samuel Clemens's larger-than-life alias. You're either dead or you're alive.

Of course, people have exaggerated stories for as long as language has been around. Whether it's the news media or "based on a true story" movies, the idea is to tell the best story possible, even if it means bending the truth a skosh.

I tend to be a bit of a storyteller myself and have been known from time to time to use hyperbole to drive a point home and give a laugh or two. But for the sake of truth-telling and transparency, I will refrain from overembellishing in this book.

Nonetheless, I think it's possible there will be moments when you will struggle to believe I could actually be so stupid. Maybe not. Maybe you bought this knowing full well how stupid I can be, and you're just here snacking on popcorn like Michael Jackson in his "Thriller" music video, watching the train crash in progress.

In fact, if you know me at all, you probably have your own cautionary tall tales of my stupidity and can attest to how many times I have "pulled a Stephen" right before your very eyes. I actually sent a text to all my friends and even asked my wife and kids, "Hey, what are the most 'Stephen' moments you can remember that I should include in my new book?" Some were a little too embarrassing *even for me* to name here, but we all had a great laugh as I got to hear their perspectives on my epic fails of olde. Or newe (everything feels cooler when you add an *e* to the ende). But something sorta clicked in my brain as I listened and I actually thought, *How am I still alive?*

Come to think of it, I think the only reason I am probably still standing now is that I have learned the art of the epic fail. It's a subtle art and not quite as elegant as some other art forms. But the beauty of it is that anyone can learn the art of the epic fail. You don't have to be born with Einstein's genius, Adele's pipes, Michael Phelps's gills and wingspan, or van Gogh's right ear. Sure, you'll have to go to school to learn the art. But this school is more of an on-the-job training situation. A school of hard knocks of sorts. But if you can learn the three tenets, you'll be a *true* artist in failing epically.

The Three Tenets of the Art of the Epic Fail

1. Failure isn't final.
2. You aren't your mistakes.
3. Your failures don't *define* you, but they can *refine* you.

Sounds simple enough, right? But if you've ever been the victim of your own failure or worse, hurt someone else, you know firsthand that this is much harder than it sounds. So at the risk of making the three tenets a little too cliché, I'll unpack them in hopes that you, my padawan learner, will someday be an adept failure artist too. Because at the end of the day, if there is one theme of truth I can use my experience to help you walk away with, it's that it's gonna be okay! No matter how bad it gets, no matter how desperate it feels or hopeless it seems, *it will be okay*.

FAILURE ISN'T FINAL

In 1921, after being fired from his job at the local newspaper for not being creative enough, a young, audacious genius started his first animation studio in the heart of the Midwest, the Laugh-O-Gram studio. Full of dreams and drive, the young man was the definition of creativity, making Laugh-O-Gram's film offerings ripe for success. There was only one problem. He was getting cheated by his distributors, and it didn't take long for his new venture to flounder, leaving the studio bankrupt in the span of just a couple of short years.

If that's not an epic fail, I don't know what is. He decided to uproot his life to the West Coast and start something fresh—a new studio that didn't play by any of the rules, but instead rewrote the whole rule book, delivering a sense of awe and wonder to everyone who encountered his work. He changed the face of entertainment in every way imaginable, creating countless iconic characters and fully immersive, multisensory-saturating experiences that burned into the imaginations of generation after generation from every nation, age, and lifestyle—even long after his death!

Fifty-nine Academy Award nominations and twenty-two wins later, the young genius said, "All the adversity I've had in my life, all my troubles and obstacles, have strengthened me . . . You may not realize it when it happens, but a kick in the teeth may be the best thing in the world for you."[4] In other words, *failure isn't final*. If you haven't guessed by now, that brilliant world-changer's name was Walt Disney.

As an avid Disney fan, I am incredibly grateful he kept going! What would I do with my seven kids on long road trips if we couldn't crank up "A Whole New World," "Circle of Life," "Into the Unknown," or "You're Welcome!" and sing along at the top of our lungs for hours on end?

Walt Disney stands alongside countless men and women who fell hard and got right back up to do something even greater than they imagined possible. Artists, athletes, and activists. Business entrepreneurs, brilliant inventors, and biochemical engineers. From Steve Jobs to Michael Jordan to Colonel Sanders, even Abraham Lincoln and Oprah, some of the greatest contributors to this big, beautiful, delicious, technologically advanced world in which we get to live have failed epically but chose not to let it be the end for them.

Thomas Edison reportedly got the light bulb right after one thousand failed attempts. You read that right. I've been hearing "third time's a charm" all my life. Saying "thousandth time's a charm" just doesn't have the same ring to it. But even after so many failures, Edison kept going.

When asked by a reporter how it felt to fail one thousand times, Edison has been famously quoted as replying, "I didn't fail 1,000 times. The light bulb was an invention with 1,000 steps."[5] Our failures are just steps to something better. Get back up and keep going. Failure isn't final. It might just be the most important step on your journey to something new.

YOU AREN'T YOUR MISTAKES

As a kid, I practically worshiped Garth Brooks. He was on the short list of my biggest musical heroes. Brilliant songwriter, genius artist, masterful performer—his music captivated the entire world with one chart-topping multiplatinum album after another, while selling out stadiums night after night. He was practically royalty in his musical genre—a larger-than-life celebrity who defined country music in the '90s. I had every tape and every song memorized down to the exact inflection and twang he used on every word. You could say I was a fan.

But in 1999, ole Garth took just a *little* detour, creating a rock star alter ego named Chris Gaines, who he hoped would help him branch out of his country music superstardom and paint with a few different colors. It was part of a larger mockumentary project, but the idea was without a doubt so outside the box that even his biggest fans didn't really take to it.

I think the main reason was that people didn't really know what to do with this new Garth Brooks. Was he Garth? Was he Chris? What was up with his hair? And makeup? Was this a joke? A midlife crisis? Why create an alter ego? And what was this music? Garth was the *king* of country, but this was nothing like his hits. And to top it all off, the whole thing was supposed to culminate in a movie that made sense of it all, yet the movie never materialized and people were left to wonder what the heck was going on with their favorite entertainer!

If you try to google Chris Gaines today, you won't find much good. While the album actually went on to be a massive commercial success[6]—eventually selling more than two million copies and reaching no. 2 on the *Billboard* 200 chart (with songs that have been covered by tons of artists, including Childish Gambino![7])—Garth said in an interview with Yahoo Music, "My ribs are still sore from getting the s*** kicked out of me for it."[8]

Yet with all that, even now if I happen to stumble into a karaoke room, you can bet your last two buffalo nickels that I'll be singing "Friends in Low Places." And so will the entire dadgum room at the top of their lungs right along with me. Garth didn't let his failure define him. He's still one of the top ten highest-paid country singers of all time! He still sells out arenas. Because he *isn't Chris Gaines*; he's *freaking Garth Brooks.*

Listen to me. You aren't your mistakes.

YOU. AREN'T. YOUR. MISTAKES.

You aren't your bankruptcy or your divorce. You aren't your broken friendships, your addictions, or your good ideas that didn't quite pan out. You aren't the five pounds you gained over the weekend or the gym membership you bought in January as a New Year's resolution but still haven't used. In fact, maybe it's time to just put down this book for a second, look yourself in the mirror right now, and say:

I'm not _____ [fill in the blank with your mistake].
I'm freaking _____ *[insert your name here]!*

Because that's what's true. To truly master the art of the epic fail, you have to practice reminding yourself that you aren't your mistakes. You have to remind yourself who you truly are. Someone who is created fearfully and wonderfully in the image of a ridiculously awesome God who loves you.[9] Completely unique. Completely wonderful.

> You have to practice reminding yourself that you aren't your mistakes.

And that's great news. Because you're going to fail! You're going to mess up! And while that doesn't mean you won't have to deal with some consequences from those failures (sometimes even devastating ones), it does mean you can learn from them, grow, and come

THE ART OF THE EPIC FAIL

out on the other end better than where you were when you started. You can let them refine you!

OUR FAILURES DON'T *DEFINE* US, BUT THEY CAN *REFINE* US!

Since failures are a given if you're going to live a life worth living at all, you should get used to learning from them! Failure is the best coach, mentor, and personal trainer your time can buy! Conversely, to put it in the words of the current fifth-richest man in the world as I write this, Bill Gates, "Success is a lousy teacher. It seduces smart people into thinking they can't lose."[10]

In his book *Creativity, Inc.*, Ed Catmull emphasizes at length that the heart of Pixar's culture and success is their insistence on failing big, beautifully, fast, and often. In almost every meeting, they're asking how they failed that week and what they learned from their failure. Rather than shying away from failure, they embrace it and grow from it because, in Ed's words, "If you aren't experiencing failure, then you are making a far worse mistake: You are being driven by the desire to avoid it."[11]

I definitely have the failing big, fast, and often thing down like a pro, though I'm not quite sure I've hit the beautiful part yet. That is, unless you consider the beautiful things that can come out of getting it wrong.

In the coming chapters, I'll be sharing a *billion* tales of my stupidity that led to my own epic fails, and all the crazy lessons I've learned along the way as a result. Okay, I promised not to exaggerate. Maybe not a billion. But probably at least thirty-two.

For every epic fail, you have at least one way you can be refined in it. Probably a lot more. In each of my failures, my goal is still to get way more out of it than I lost from it. Whether it's learning to be a little kinder with your words or growing in your gratitude. Or maybe it's learning that, yes, the speed limits do apply to you. Maybe it's learning to slow down or be more patient with yourself and with others. Or perhaps it's just learning that you actually matter. You have value and worth that is greater than you could have ever imagined. I've had to learn all of these, and much more, the hard way by employing the art of the epic fail.

I wish I could say I'm good to go now! But the truth is, I probably still have an *actual* billion epic fails left in my lifetime. And while that may seem a bit disheartening at first consideration, it's actually encouraging. Because if I can truly master this art of failing epically, it means growing even more. More refinement. And the Stephen you'll meet a year from today will be much better than the Stephen who is sitting here writing these words.

We are all on our own journey, and despite the cancel culture in which we live, people are people everywhere you go. Fallible. Hypocritical. Hypercritical. Holier-than-thou about our morality (religious, political, or otherwise), and utterly in need of grace.

Maybe, just maybe, our failures will make us humble enough to have authentic—not contrived or calculated—mercy, empathy, and compassion for one another and for ourselves. Maybe when we fall down and get back up enough times, we will start to see a pattern that no matter how bad it gets, it really is gonna be okay.

I recently became obsessed with the TV show *Ted Lasso*. Not because I'm obsessed with soccer—or as the rest of the world calls it, football. We just *have* to be different, so we call it soccer and have a completely different sport called football. Much like using pounds or Fahrenheit or miles. Why do we have to make everything so dang confusing? But, alas, Americans are rebels who love to reinvent the wheel, I suppose.

I think the runaway success of *Ted Lasso* may be attributed to his seemingly boundless capacity for hope during a season when I think we'd all agree we need more hope. It can come across as naive or even foolish at times, but his contagious brand of optimism just has a way of turning the tide even on the darkest of days and worst of mess-ups. It softens the hardest, most cynical heart. It encourages the most down-trodden, who are thinking to themselves, *Dear God, what have I done? Am I done?*

You failed? No problem. Try again. You got it all wrong *again*? Cool deal. Just another step to getting it right. "You know what the happiest animal is? The goldfish. You know why? It's got a ten-second memory."[12]

Feels a bit oversimplistic when we try to overthink it. But compared to the alternative of endlessly wallowing in our failures and letting them paralyze us from being able to move forward, I'm gonna choose to be a goldfish, get the heck back up, and keep kicking.

Our failures teach us resilience. They help us reframe our perspective without rewriting the truth. Not just moving on from how we got it wrong, but moving forward with the hard-won wisdom we earned from our mess-up.

No matter how badly we may have missed the mark, the sun is still gonna rise and paint the sky with a million glorious hues of grace—as though God were screaming out, *It's gonna be okay. I've got this. I haven't forgotten you. I'm still faithful. Just trust me!*

That's not a trite statement of naive optimism or blind faith. That's not me being a giddy cheerleader covering my eyes and ears and shouting cute little things. That's spiritual truth backed by scientific, albeit poetic, fact. This day may go on to be the crappiest day of your life thus far. But in spite of how big all that's going on in your world feels and may be, the world is so much bigger than you or me, and there are a million breathtaking things happening right this very minute that infuse all of our chaos with meaning, even if we can't quite locate the meaning yet.

Your chaos is different from my chaos. But chaos is chaos, and no matter who you are, we all have days where we feel like we can't catch a break or catch our breath. And those are the moments when we have to reframe our perspective and embrace the hope of this truth: *No matter how bad our world gets, there is always more beauty than brokenness.*

> No matter how bad our world gets, there is always more beauty than brokenness.

I happen to be a Christian, so while I'm writing from a faith-filled worldview, I'm not trying to shove anything down anyone's throat or force my faith on anyone.

I am not holier than thou art. I am holier than literally no one art.

But it is precisely *because* of my faith that I can look at the valley of dry bones, the rubble of my past mistakes, and all the brutal things that have happened to me, stand up, wipe the blood and sweat from my brow, and know beyond a doubt that it really will be okay. Someone far stronger, wiser, kinder, and more loving than I could ever imagine is working it all together for my good. Because Jesus himself carried all those mistakes to the cross and died there for them, and for me, I can trust he is making everything okay.

My failures don't define me because he already has. My mistakes aren't my identity because he's already given me a better identity. No matter how wrong Woody got it, at the end of the day Andy was still the name on the bottom of his boot. And I have a better name than Andy written on mine.

Maybe you're not there yet. I totally get it. I've been there too.

Even now, I have more question marks than exclamation points floating around in my head about faith and God and life and everything in between. There is far more I don't understand than I do.

I don't know why we suffer, but we all do. If you've been alive longer than three minutes, you know this to be true.

I don't know why bad things happen, but they happen to all of us—the good, the bad, and the ugly. (Except none of us are ugly. We are, after all, beautiful people!)

But what I do know is that in every instance, my suffering has taught me patient endurance, like a scalpel cutting out all the junk and showing me all the stuff I had been putting my hope in that can never truly satisfy me. And most of the mistakes I've made have been the result of hoping and trusting in the wrong things.

In those moments, I come to a crossroads on what to believe. I can be tempted to let my failures define me. Lord knows, other people will try to define me by my failures. It's human nature. Maybe it helps us feel better about ourselves to reduce other people to their biggest mistakes. Feels like a weird way to get worth for yourself at the expense of others, but we're all tempted to do it at times.

A CASE OF MISTAKEN IDENTITY

Everyone is always trying to give you an identity. But that's not who you truly are. I've had more cases of mistaken identity in my life than I can even count.

My whole life, I've been called the Space Cowboy. (Thank you, Steve Miller Band.) At every introduction, people ask me if I'm a joker, smoker, or midnight toker. For the record, I am none of the above, though *The Dark Knight* is to this day one of the best movies ever and

THE ART OF GETTING IT WRONG

I do love to smoke a good brisket from time to time. Plus, I actually do wanna fly like an eagle.

Having a name like Stephen Miller comes with its unique set of challenges, and I have considered changing my name more times than I can count. But I'm in too deep now to turn back! Maybe I'll just create a superstar alter ego named something rad like Benedict Cumberbatch—mainly because it's the most fun name on earth to say and I don't think I'd get confused with anyone else.

When we were adopting Penelope and Lincoln from China, one day my Twitter started blowing up with super-hateful tweets directed at me—the verified @StephenMiller—calling me the most atrocious names and saying the most outrageously terrible things to me. I learned that week that I'm a vampire Nazi whose family deserves to be murdered, and that I look like a giant big toe whose mom should have drowned me as a baby. And that is just the PG-rated sampling. I was completely blindsided and couldn't figure out why all this shade was getting thrown at me!

Turns out, there was another Stephen Miller in the world I was getting mixed up with! This is not surprising since, in a world of, like, eight billion people, close to one billion of them are named Stephen Miller. But this particular Stephen Miller was working in the White House and had just done an interview on a news show. People were outraged at him, to put it mildly. So I decided to put that little case of mistaken identity to good use! I tweeted, "If everyone throwing shade at me right now would donate to help bring our kids home from China, we might actually get some good done with all this! #LoveWins"

It was such a ludicrous situation that it got covered by the local news and then shared by news stations all over the country. A few of the haters figured out they had a case of mistaken identity and were ruthlessly seeking to destroy the wrong Stephen Miller, and they were moved by our story, so we raised $2,500 that day toward our adoption fees!

But the best case of mistaken identity happened to me in 2014. I was in over my head, feeling like I was drowning, struggling to provide for five kids on a pastor's salary, which looks a lot like being the ringleader of a circus, only without the booming baritone voice of Hugh Jackman or the bulging biceps and astounding acrobatics of Zac Efron. So I decided to try my hand at Uber driving to make some cash on the side. We were living in Austin, Texas, at the time and I'd heard you could really rake in the cash driving for South by Southwest, the Austin City Limits Music Festival, and all the other amazing stuff they had going on all the time.

I waited and waited to be approved as a driver, only to have my visions of diving into a giant vault of gold coins like Scrooge McDuck interrupted by a surprising letter turning me down as a driver. Apparently I had a warrant for my arrest in Michigan for assaulting an officer, perpetrating arson, and *committing murder*. I called to insist that this was a mistake and that they had the wrong guy.

They meticulously looked over all the paperwork and found that the Stephen Miller in question was not in fact Stephen Daniel Miller but Stephen David Miller, and they were looking at a case of mistaken identity.

Just when I thought this would be the last I would hear of the other Stephen Miller, I was pulled over a week later in Louisiana because I suppose a bunch of dudes in a Suburban pulling a white trailer looked sus.

My band and I had just come from leading worship at a student event and had a wad of cash in the door that kinda fell out when the officer asked me to step out of the car.

"That's just from selling merch to a bunch of kids." I said as he patted me down, not realizing how bad that sounded to a cop who thinks I'm probably a drug dealer.

"Oh really?" he said. "I'm gonna need to see your ID and insurance."

I handed it to him, and he had me sit on the grass on the side of the road as his partner searched our trailer and interviewed the band guys one by one. Then the cop came back and very nervously asked with his hand on his holstered gun, "Stephen, when's the last time you were in Michigan?"

"I've never been to Michigan, sir."

"Well, there's a warrant for your arrest in Michigan for assault of an officer, arson, and murder."

I laughed with one of those extremely nervous laughs, trying to hide the paralyzing fear that was overwhelming me inside. "Sir, I have a funny story about that. Turns out there are 3,000,000,482 Stephen Millers in the world, of which 119,000 have *D* as a middle initial and it just so happens that there is a Stephen David Miller in Michigan who wrecked my shot at being an Uber driver last week, and I'm guessing that's the guy you're looking for, but it ain't me. I'm still a little sore about it, so if you need any additional proof of identification, I'm more than happy to provide it, but you got the wrong guy."

He laughed as he walked back to the car before coming back to let us go on our way with a "Your left taillight is out on the trailer. Get that fixed."

You could say that was pretty stressful. I think I lost forty-two of my best hair follicles that day.

But the crazy thing about it is that no matter how much people tried to tell me I was Stephen David Miller, someone running from the law for assault, arson, and murder, I'm not Stephen David Miller. I'm Stephen Daniel Miller. People don't get to give me someone else's identity. That's not their job. That's not their right.

It's the same with our mistakes. No matter how much people try to brand us by how we got it wrong, that's not their job. That's not their right.

Sure, a consequence of our actions will shape the way some people see us. It may change how much freedom we have in certain situations, possibly even our entire future. Certainly, if I were an *actual* murderer, there would have been a drastically different outcome in my encounter with the police or with Uber.

I'm not saying we don't have to deal with the ramifications of our epic fails. But I am saying that while they can inform us, they don't get to define who we are. And sometimes the consequence shapes us more than the mistake itself.

Our failures don't get to rob us of the identity and purpose we've already been given by God. They may actually push us further into that purpose.

After all, he's the one who more or less originally wrote the tenets of the art of the epic fail. I'm just trying to steal his ideas, but I'm pretty sure they're public domain, so if you don't tell, neither will I.

Your failure isn't final. You aren't your mistakes. Your failures don't *define* you, but they can *refine* you.

Let's learn to be epic fail artists together. Cause there is so much life on the other side.

CHAPTER 3

STICKS AND STONES MAY BREAK MY BONES, BUT WORDS MIGHT JACK ME UP FOREVER

W hat is it about the song you don't like?"

I stared at my new boss (you know, the guy who approves my paychecks and consequently my ability to provide for my giant army of kids—that guy) across the room, keenly aware that my next words could be my last as an employee at this particular church. "I mean . . . you know . . . I just think it could be better."

"Yeah, sure, but like, what could be better about it?"

We went round and round for what felt like an eternity, though in reality it was only seconds, and I began doing mental gymnastics to find the most inoffensive way to express an intangible feeling like musical/lyrical preference, but before I could stop myself, the words vomited from my lips like projectile weapons, ruthlessly making their way to my own destruction.

"Okay, if you really wanna know, I think the lyrics sound like something my eight-year-old would write."

Oh crud. Did I actually just say that? The world moved in slow motion as he lifted his head at a rate that made my heart beat a thousand miles a minute.

"Oh."

The sheer speed of backpedaling I attempted in that moment would probably have won me the Tour de France in reverse against a dopeless Lance Armstrong seven times out of seven.

Somehow we managed to patch things up, largely because he was much more gracious than I was, but to say we got off to a rocky start would be massively understated.

CAN I GET A FILTER?

Some people have a "filter." It's that mental muscle that keeps you from saying *exactly* what you're thinking. I don't seem to have one of those. Unsurprisingly, it's gotten me in trouble more times than I can count.

Like the time I told my wife in the middle of a heated argument not to yell because, and I quote, "It's not becoming of you." It's a wonder I'm still alive. But that is completely credited to her long-suffering compassion toward me. And maybe slightly influenced by the fact that I give good massages.

Amanda is one of those women who just knows how to love people well. She has an unparalleled gift of hospitality and it's one of the ways we really complement each other. She is an incredible host who thinks of the smallest details, down to having fresh flowers, cute serving trays, and just the right stemless wineglasses for her signature sangria that will change your life forever.

As an extrovert who loves to cook, I love this about her more than I even know how to describe. Together, we have so much fun entertaining and hosting people for a great meal and conversation.

For the majority of our parenting life, we've been the youngsters with kiddos, babies raising babies, and most of our friends were barely even married, without kids even on the tip of their brains yet. So when we finally had some friends over with kids who were pretty close to our own children's ages, we were a bit giddy.

After a delicious meal of chicken manicotti, Caesar salad, and garlic bread, the conversation and sangria were flowing, and so were the laughs. One of their daughters came up and was having a bit of a bad night, and in the way kids do, she expressed that to her mom in a way that made me think of a movie.

"Have you guys seen *Wedding Crashers*?" (Sidenote: I don't endorse this movie, but my brain acts as a sponge, and I remember movie quotes better than my own birthday.)

My sweet, thoughtful, mindful, aware Amanda was now on high alert. After having been with me for a decade at that point, she knew exactly how my thought process worked—a miracle in and of itself, since I still don't—and she knew where my mind was going. I was, however, much less aware of the light squeeze of my hand acting as a warning sign to engage my filter and not continue with my current stream of thought. We were on a collision course with awkwardness.

"Yeah, it's hilarious!"

"You know the part where Vince Vaughn is making balloon animals?"

"Yeeeessss?"

"Your daughter just reminded me of the kid who was like, 'Make me a bicycle, clown!'"

Nervous laughter ensued. No one but me thought it was funny. I didn't even realize it was just about the dumbest thing I could have said. Luckily, I was informed that it was, and I had the opportunity to apologize. Not sure how you really come back from that. But thankfully, we are still friends with this amazing family to this day and, just for fun, I'm often reminded of how awkward that first dinner together was.

When it comes to words, we don't have the option of putting the proverbial toothpaste back in the tube. But we can choose what we do with them once they're out there. And how we respond to even the dumbest statements may just give us a prettier smile when all is said and done.

THE DARK SIDE OF THE FORCE

Of course, I never think I'm being rude. I'm a pretty jovial guy who never really stops smiling. I just love to smile. Smiling's my favorite. See, there it is again. Only this time, a much better Will Ferrell movie.

But even with the joyful visage that comes from being a genuinely happy guy pretty much all the time, I have learned over the years the not-so-subtle art of sarcasm to get my point across, and as much as I think it's delivering the blow as softly as possible, it often just adds salt to the proverbial wound.

One Sunday morning a few years back, I was working with a band at a church, and we were running a song that for whatever reason, we just couldn't seem to get right. No matter how much we woodshedded it, it just wasn't coming together.

Having played with my own band thousands of times, I had grown accustomed to a level of excellence that is probably unrealistic to expect from most church worship teams. Unfortunately, as my passion for excellence increased, my patience for unprepared and underperforming players was pretty much nonexistent at this point.

"Stop stop stop stop stop!" I exclaimed, bringing the song to a screeching halt.

"I'm not sure what's going on here, guys, but this just isn't working."

Then turning to the guitar player, I drew from my vast database of movie quotes and moments and, with the sincerest of lighthearted intentions, tried my best to express my deep desire to get this song right.

"You know in *Star Wars* when Palpatine looks over at Luke and then just starts shooting him with blue lightning from his fingertips?"

"Yeah?" the guitar player said.

"You know how Luke doubles over on the ground and is just screaming and crying because it hurts so much?"

"Yeah?" he said, a little more confused.

"That screaming pain he felt must have been so intense for him, don't you think?"

"Yeah?"

"Well, that's pretty much exactly how I feel inside right now because you keep missing like pretty much all the notes and I feel like it's sort of making my soul double over in agony. Do you think you can get it right, or do we need to just skip this one and do a different song?"

As an avid *Star Wars* fan, he was sort of nervously grinning up to this point, and I watched as his smile slowly melted into utter dejection. I had gotten my point across, but at what cost? Certainly not without him feeling I had mortally wounded his heart.

Turns out *I* was Palpatine, not the other way around.

As he hung his head, utterly discouraged, I turned to the band and said, "Guys, I'm so sorry. That was below the belt. I should have been more careful with my words there. You guys are amazing, and I love you all."

Then turning back to my guitar player, "Dude, I'm so sorry. I don't know what the heck I was thinking. That was totally wrong to say that. I got ahead of myself and was so focused on the music being good that I really failed to lead and love you guys well. Let's scrap the song, and we can do something we know a little better. I'm so incredibly sorry. Please forgive me."

I'm so glad he did forgive me. He went on to become a great friend whom I still love to this day. He really buckled down on his practicing to become quite an incredible player, even traveling with my band from time to time. But a lesser man may not have let that be our story. I'm truly grateful for his humility and maturity.

I generally think I'm fairly self-aware. But then I start writing down memories like this and realize just how unaware I really am.

My wife informs me right now as I read this to her that pretty much by now everyone probably thinks I'm a big fat jerk and that most of the reviews of this book (Oh, by the way, please leave a review of this book on Amazon. Thank you!) are going to be, "Wow, this guy is kind of a butt." And up until, like, three minutes ago, I kinda thought I was a pretty good guy. So much for self-awareness.

At the same time, lest I become just a bit too self-flagellatory, I have to believe I'm not alone in this. Like, I'm not trying to dodge a bullet or self-soothe here, but the Bible does have a few things to say about the power of our words. Take James 3:2–8, for example, which soberly reminds us:

> We all stumble in many ways. Anyone who is never at fault in what they say is perfect, able to keep their whole body in check.
>
> When we put bits into the mouths of horses to make them obey us, we can turn the whole animal. Or take ships as an example. Although they are so large and are driven by strong winds, they are steered by a very small rudder wherever the pilot wants to go. Likewise, the tongue is a small part of the body, but it makes great boasts. Consider what a great forest is set on fire by a small spark. The tongue also is a fire, a world of evil among the parts of the body. It corrupts the whole body, sets the whole course of one's life on fire, and is itself set on fire by hell.
>
> All kinds of animals, birds, reptiles and sea creatures are being tamed and have been tamed by mankind, but no human being can tame the tongue. It is a restless evil, full of deadly poison.

I don't think James is really overstating things here. Feels to me like he is just expanding on Proverbs 18:21, which reads, "The tongue has the power of life and death."

Translation—sticks and stones may break my bones, but words may jack someone's life up forever. Don't underestimate the power of your words. Be careful how you talk to people. Be mindful how what you say can hurt or heal.

You don't have to believe what I believe about God or share my perspective on almost anything at all to know that this is true. Our words really do matter. Deeply. Profoundly.

DON'T GET BLOOD ON THE CARPET

As I was growing up, I got in a fight what felt like every day. As the overweight kid, I was ridiculed and bullied incessantly, sometimes through physical aggression, sometimes with words from which I still have scars to this day.

"Hey, Tubby!"

"Hey, Fatty!"

Or my personal favorite—"Hey, Titties!" Very original. Because, you know, I was overweight, so I had man boobs. Kids are witty.

I always loved going to the public swimming pool because without fail, I was asked if I was a boy or a girl. It didn't help that my voice didn't get lower until I was a senior in high school, making my "I'm a boy" response fairly unconvincing.

In middle school gym class, kids would throw rocks at me and scream, "Run faster, Titties! I bet if we put a donut in front of him, he'd run faster!"

As a fairly tenderhearted kid, I would kindly turn to them and ask them to stop, to which they would respond, "Whatcha gonna do? Sit on us?"

One day on the school bus coming home from a school field trip, an eighth-grade star football player who was a good foot taller than me walked up to my seat and said, "Hey, Fatty, you're in my seat. Move. Now."

As a defense mechanism, I had become an adept artisan of sarcasm by this point, so I slowly looked up at him and said in the most confident voice I could muster, "I may be fat, but you're ugly. I can always lose weight, but you're always gonna be ugly. Sorry, dude. Tough life. Maybe the school counselor can help you work through the pain of it all."

The moment we stepped off the bus, I knew I needed to get outta there. I walked as fast as I could to the water fountain and tried to play it cool like I was unfazed. But as soon as that first drip of water touched my lips, I felt the jarring pain of this kid's right fist against my right cheekbone.

Whack! Boom! Pow! (I imagine it sounded like the old Adam West *Batman* TV show.)

My cheek was on fire after three consecutive blows. I knew I couldn't win this fight. There was no way. But you don't always have to win with fists. Sometimes words can suffice. I pretended to not notice the punching, finished taking my drink, slowly lifted my head with a smirk that hurt more than I would ever let on, and said, "Really, bro? Is that seriously the hardest you can hit? I honestly thought you would be a pretty strong guy, but man. Maybe go hit up the gym and come back to me when you know how to throw a punch."

The hubris. But it worked. He was stunned by my words to the point that I had a few short moments to walk away to the principal's office and call my parents to come get me. I could see the boys staring at me through the window, gasping at my obviously swollen cheek. Good thing it was Friday and I would have a few days for the bruising to heal before returning to school. Good thing my dad's only rule about fighting was, "If you're gonna fight, you better win."

My mom added an amendment to this law: "Don't get blood on the carpet." Smart lady. You never get your rent deposit back in real life, especially when there are bloodstains on the carpet.

I never lost a fight. But the words that some of those bullies said to me still haunted me even into my late thirties. In 2003, I lost a hundred pounds and have fought hard year after year to keep it off because I wanted to "show them." Sure, there are a ton of health benefits. Sure, I feel better about myself when I look in the mirror and like the way my clothes fit. Sure, I wanna be around for my wife and kiddos and eventually grandkiddos. I already have my grandpa name picked out— Pops! But I know that deep down inside, I'm always fighting against being the fat kid who everyone bullied. The words left deep scars that have driven me.

I have fought the urge toward workaholism my entire adult life, and I know that some of that is subconsciously driven by a need to prove that I'm not the fat kid everyone bullied growing up. I'm not the kid they threw rocks at. I'm not the kid they dumped their Cokes on and shoved into the locker. I'm not the boy all the girls checked "no" for on the "check yes or no" questionnaire I gave them.

I know this is true. I have a gorgeous wife who is glowing with entire universes worth of light and beauty. She's witty and brilliant and absolutely hilarious and chooses to love me despite knowing all my deepest, darkest places of brokenness. She encourages me and challenges me and makes me a better man every day. I have seven unbelievably cool kids who love me and think I'm a pretty great dad! I enjoy every single moment I get to have with them and have had that privilege for almost two decades.

I've been fairly successful at just about everything I've tried my hand at—from running snow cone stands, pizza shops, and rodeo arenas to worship leading, songwriting, and photography. Heck, I even did a stint selling tractor implements and didn't do too shabby!

And I truly love what I'm blessed to get to do now! I have a job that has connected me to an insanely supportive community on YouTube that genuinely cares about my family and wants to see us thrive.

Beyond that, I am completely known and completely loved by a God who gave his only Son, Jesus, so I could walk in freedom with joy and peace, adopted into his family forever and loved unconditionally.

I have *nothing* to prove. But the painful words that haunt me surely tempt me to feel like I do. Words might jack me up forever.

SCARS ON YOUR HEART

You probably have those words and phrases that have stuck with you as well. That have left scars on your heart and are branded into your mind. That make you wince, even decades after hearing them. Maybe from a teacher. Maybe from a parent or a spouse. Maybe you've been through counseling to help you heal from them because as much as you don't want them to affect you, you can't deny that they have and do.

The good news is, you aren't the painful words that were spoken to you. They don't define you, but they can refine you. Rather than allowing the words spoken to you to derail your life, you can learn from them, grow from them, and become better because of them. You can metabolize them as fuel for your journey.

The same is true about the words we've allowed to flow from our own lips. There's power in them. Power to be a life dealer or a death dealer. You may have strung together a few phrases that haunt someone else to this day. You may have wounded them in ways you don't yet know and maybe even they don't fully understand. Maybe you've got your own Emperor Palpatine moments.

But it's never too late, as far as it's up to you, to make it right. No matter how badly you got it wrong.

I started mowing and raking lawns when I was eight to try to help provide for my family because we were dirt-poor. I think something about that made me want to always try to be the hardest worker in the room. All through high school, I held down jobs to help my mom keep food on the table after my dad left. I didn't mind working and helping out. In some ways I think it caused me to grow up a little more quickly than maybe I would have otherwise. But in other ways, it bent me toward an immature pride that made me feel like I deserved better. I would never have said as much, but it was there.

> It's never too late, as far as it's up to you, to make it right.

So when I was twenty years old and found out my boss was making $50,000 a year while I was pulling in a lousy $100 a week, I was pretty livid. Granted, I was a total novice and my job was only two days a week, while he had spent longer than I had been alive paying his dues and honing his craft, and he was running the entire operation. But I didn't have the perspective for that. I felt I was being cheated.

I was really good at what I did and wasn't being recognized for the value I brought to the table. So I wrote him a scathing email message: "I feel like I'm working like crazy and putting in all this time to make this place as amazing as I can and I'm making a lousy hundred dollars a week while you pull down fifty thousand a year! I need a raise. You're taking advantage of me, and I won't stand for it."

I was such a dumb kid with so much to learn. He was giving me a shot at getting started. He was teaching me and training me and showing me the way. I had climbed a total of literally zero mountains in life and wanted to be treated like I had conquered Everest.

I think back to those pompous, cocky words I wrote and cringe.

About fifteen years later, I ran into my old boss, and he was cordial to me, smiling and shaking my hand. We caught up for a few minutes and exchanged numbers. And as I was driving home, that email came to mind. I actually began crying because of how deeply regretful I was over it. Once I parked the car, I sat there in the driver's seat and composed a text to him.

Hey brother. So good seeing you today. I just wanted to take a minute and apologize for something. You may not even remember me writing this, but when I was working for you, I wrote you a pretty unacceptable email accusing you of taking advantage of me. I was harsh and immature, and I'm so sorry. Please forgive me. I wouldn't be where I am today without you having given me a chance to learn and grow and build my skills. You were kind and gracious and patient with me when I most definitely did not deserve it. I just wanted to say thank you and let you know how much you mean to me and how much you have impacted my life.

As I hit Send, I felt relief wash over me. I was choosing not to let my failure define me or my relationship with my old boss. But it was refining me. And it was gonna be okay.

He wrote back,

Hey, man! I forgive you. No question about it. No strings attached. I honestly didn't even remember that until your text, but thinking back, that really did hurt because I was genuinely trying to help you and my family was actually struggling financially at the time, so it was a little bit of another blow I wasn't expecting. It's amazing to see the man you've become, and I'm glad I got to be part of that. Grateful for you and glad we had that moment today. And thankful for this healing text. Love you, brother.

Words can wound. Words can heal. Even if you've used your words as weapons, your failure isn't final. No matter how badly you got it wrong, it's never too late to make things right.

THE WEIGHT OF EVERY SYLLABLE

Any time Justin Bieber's "Sorry" comes on the radio, one of two things is destined to happen every single time:

1. I will break out in the Obama rendition where some brilliant editor hunted tirelessly for clips from all his speeches and strung them together to make him sing the song. It's hilarious, and once you've seen it, you can't unsee it. It will forever define that song for you.
2. I will replace the words "your body" with "Pilates" because the kids are in the car and I'd rather they think about the value of fitness and health. And definitely *not* someone's body. Not yet anyway.

But the hook of the song is "Is it too late now to say sorry?"[13] and the answer is emphatically, "No!"

No matter how much OneRepublic and Timbaland conspire to lie to you, it's never "too late to apologize."[14]

Now, to be fair, the person to whom you are apologizing may not be ready to receive it or forgive you. Words cut deep, and people heal on their own timelines. You can't force it or rush it. And they don't owe you anything. Not forgiveness. Not closure. Nothing. But that's where the key phrase "so far as it's up to you" comes in. You can't make someone heal. But you can be an agent of reconciliation by giving them words of life that can help them choose healing.

I think at most people's core, they don't want to be wallowing in their pain from the hurtful words spoken to them. I know I don't want to! I'm sure you don't either! Most of us just need that little nudge to help us forgive and find peace.

But if I had to guess, a lot of people are walking around with unhealed wounds and will never get half the apologies they deserve or need to hear. You are probably one of those people. So am I. If we ourselves need apologies, wouldn't we want to be people who give them to others, both for their sakes and for our own? I think the world would be a lot safer place if we did.

We are all gonna say things we don't mean sometimes, or even things we do mean but we haven't fully considered the ramifications of letting them loose on someone else. We will wound and torture others with our carelessly expressed thoughts. That's part of being human. We all get it wrong sometimes.

Hear me now: you are not the hurtful things you have said. The careless words you have spoken are not the *final* word. The pain you may have caused doesn't define you, but it can refine you!

As I get older, after failing at this more times than I can count, I'm trying my best to slow down and count the cost of my words. I'm learning the weight of every syllable and sound, the consequences of every consonant and vowel.

There's an old adage that God gave us two ears and one mouth so that we would listen twice as much as we speak. I'm finding this to be true now more than ever. Going back to the wisdom of James, "Everyone should be quick to listen, slow to speak and slow to become angry" (James 1:19).

I'm learning to listen far more than I speak. Encourage far more than I criticize. Build up far more than I tear down. Keep my thoughts to myself every once in a while. Not need to know everything or fix everything.

I still stink at it. But these days, I'm trying not to be defensive when I mess up. I would rather admit my failure as quickly as possible and ask for forgiveness the first chance I get.

I want to be a life dealer with my words.

CHAPTER 4

IF YOU KEEP PUTTING IT OFF, IT'S JUST GONNA SUCK MORE

I might have a *slight* case of ADHD. Combine that with a dreamer-type, lack-of-detail orientation and a general stubbornness that keeps me from doing things I don't like to do, and sometimes I can let things go *just a little* too long.

Like the time I waited to renew my car registration for two years and it cost me $700 instead of $40! That shoulda taught me, right? Except that literally as I write this, my registration has been expired for like four months. Truth is, I just don't want to make it a priority to get it done because it's not fun and I have better things to do. I actually put a mental block in my brain to forget that I need to do it because I'm working it up in my mind that it's gonna suck so badly.

I'm gonna be in line for 123 years and have to talk to some blue-haired woman who hates her job and yells at me and the cops are gonna drag me out of the office and impound my car. Okay, maybe it wouldn't be that bad. But it's funny how our minds play tricks on us and induce anxiety tilted toward the worst-case scenario.

The reality of getting done the stuff we need to do is rarely as bad as our anxiety builds it up in our minds to be.

Funny thing was it took me only ten minutes to have an extremely friendly woman tell me it was only going to be $700 and I was in and out at record speed. If I had just gone in a year earlier, it would have taken ten minutes for that sweet woman to tell me it was only $40. The reality of getting done the stuff we need to do is rarely as bad as our anxiety builds it up in our minds to be.

A few months ago, I made a TikTok that sorta poked fun at my kids (with their permission, of course, because I try my best not to be a terrible dad), pretending to be them calling in an order for pizza delivery and basically begging God for no one to pick up because they have too much anxiety to actually talk to someone on the phone, even if the proverbial pot of gold on the other end of the rainbow is, as Kevin McCallister says, "A lovely cheese pizza just for me."[15]

Freaking out, hyperventilating: "Please don't pick up. Please don't pick up . . . PLEASE GOD, DON'T PICK UP!"

Tone abruptly changes to chipper and cheery: "Hi, yes! I'd like to order a pizza for delivery!"

The reality was nowhere near what their anxiety had built it up in their heads to be. Our minds play tricks on us in the most humorous ways.

As it turned out, I got hundreds of messages from teens—"This is so me!" And almost as many from parents—"This is so my kid!"

How do we allow our minds to do this to us? We really don't believe it's gonna be okay. We worry and fret and build it up and minimize it all at once, and we end up missing out. Of course, not everything is as simple as ordering pizza. But the same truth applies to ordering Jimmy John's too. Or having a hard conversation with someone. Or getting a leaky faucet fixed.

IT WAS JUST A LITTLE DRIP

We used to have a home with the most glorious backyard deck on it. Like *Better Homes & Gardens* magazine kind of good. The kind we had always dreamed of. Huge trees shading it. A slide off the back down to the trampoline. String lights crisscrossed overhead. Jasmine vines lining the lattice. And a dinner table big enough for our gigantic family.

As much as humanly possible in the more than one hundred days of over-100-degree heat of Texas, we spent most of our waking hours out on that thing, from breakfast to dinner to reading and even outdoor movie nights, complete with projector, screen, blankets, and popcorn. It was our favorite place.

One of our kids' favorite pastimes was to hook up the water hose to the little spigot on the deck and run it down to the trampoline with a sprinkler attached. They would play and play until they passed out at night, only to literally rinse and repeat the next day.

One morning I was out on the back deck reading, basking under the warmth of a cloudless sky, the cool breeze brushing against my skin. It was heavenly. But being a person who is easily what I call "audibly distracted," my attention kept getting pulled away by a soft, subtle dripping sound. Nothing crazy. But it was rhythmic. Consistent. Every couple seconds, just a light drip onto the wooden deck. It was starting to pool, but nothing terrible. I assumed the kids hadn't screwed on the hose quite tight enough and it would be fine. Nothing that really required any sort of action on my part in that moment.

The next morning as I completed my morning workout on the back deck, the dripping continued. I gave the hose a good turn onto the spigot—righty tighty, lefty loosey, right? Right. Job done. Mission accomplished. I'm so good at fixing things. I deserve a major award. Maybe a bowling alley. But I'd settle for a leg lamp.

The truth is, I am terrible at fixing things. I'm the king of leaving the furniture in the box for months after we ordered it because I am dreading the last step of putting it together, where I realize I missed a step at the very beginning and have to take it all apart and start over.

And I have the added bonus of hearing a voice in my head (I promise

I'm not crazy) saying, "You can't force it! Stop trying to force it! You're gonna break it!" Apparently brute force isn't usually the answer. I have found this out the hard way on more than one occasion.

So this was my rationalization that I was doing what I needed to do so I could feel better about myself, while my subconscious pushed away thoughts of my lack of, shall we say, proficiency in solving plumbing problems.

The next day, the drip was a little worse. And the next. And the next. *Procrastination much?*

I really need to fix that, I kept saying to make myself feel productive as I walked past the spigot every day. But I was actually pretty anxious about doing it wrong. Breaking it worse. Calling a plumber and being charged $2,500 to have them come out. Or worse, there coulda been some broken pipe behind the brick, and we'd have to rip it all up and replace all the piping. My fears got irrational pretty quickly. So the drip got worse.

Now I never vocalized it. I don't even know that I knew how much I was rationalizing away my fears with the passive procrastination of *I really need to fix that.*

We left for a couple weeks' adventure to the Grand Canyon, and I vowed to myself that I would fix it as soon as we got back. I even made a reminder on my phone to call someone to help me fix it on the day we returned. And I did. Because as soon as we got home, I realized what a bad idea it was not to have fixed the leak before leaving. The drip had become a steady stream, and the wooden beams underneath it were starting to look like they were rotting. Buckling. Deteriorating. Discolored. I needed to act fast.

I called my friend Colin, who is just an all-around handyman who seems like he can pretty much do anything and everything. Did I mention he also plays guitar like a beast, has a super-rad beard, and has arms that are sleeved with some of the most kick-butt tattoos I've ever seen to round out his Most Interesting Man in the World persona? He's the guy I called anytime I needed to build or fix anything. And not just cause I couldn't get ahold of the Dos Equis guy.

"Hey, dude, I need some help. I've got a pretty bad leak on a spigot in the back. For like a month now. And I'm not sure how to fix it." I sent him a few pics, and he dropped by Home Depot on the way to my house to pick up a replacement spigot. He pulled up with an eight-dollar part and pair of channel lock pliers, and within five minutes, the drip was fixed. Colin had saved the day.

Wow, that wasn't nearly as bad as I thought it would be. I really dodged a bullet there.

Then the water bill came in, and the other shoe dropped with a thud heard round the world.

Before I tell you the amount, let me tell you, the world's smallest violin started playing just for me the moment I opened that envelope. Nothing could have prepared me for having the wind knocked out of me like that.

Two thousand five hundred dollars. I had to type that out because $2,500 just doesn't have the same effect. Two. Thousand. Five. Hundred. Dollars. Of water. A simple compound of two hydrogen molecules and one oxygen molecule that covers roughly 71 percent of the earth's surface. That must have been some high quality H_2O slowly dripping little by little for a month, because—and I repeat—*twenty-five hundred dollars*! All because I kept saying, *I really need to fix that* instead of actually doing the dang thing.

These are the things we don't film for YouTube. Mainly because I'm not ready for that kind of embarrassment. So I'll just put it in this book and hope for the best, trusting that someone can learn a little sump'n from my epic fails. Getting it wrong can be quite expensive sometimes.

ALLOW ME TO BE BLUNT

As a dad, I'm always coming up with little reminder statements to help my kids remember big life lessons easily. "Procrastination leads to devastation" feels artsy to me at first glance, but upon further consideration, it sounds a bit like a Southern Baptist preacher's idea of catchy when they make it their first of three points in their thirty-three-minute sermon. It just doesn't have the same punch or ring to it as, "If you keep putting it off, it's just gonna suck more."

All dads do this. When I was dating Amanda, every time I was getting ready to take her out, her dad would look at her and say, "Make good choices." Then quickly he'd turn to me, scowl, and say, "Don't do anything with her you wouldn't do with your grandma."

Sometimes bluntness just works better.

So allow me to be blunt. You've got something in your life right now that you know you just need to go ahead and do. Writing the paper. Doing your taxes. Having the hard conversation. Scheduling an appointment with a therapist because you're on the verge of a midlife crisis. Getting serious about paying off your credit card debt so your finances are freed up. Calling the doctor to get that growth checked out. Whatever it might be. It might suck a lot! But I can tell you first-hand, if you keep putting it off, it's just gonna suck more.

When I look at all the moments in my life when putting off decisions and people and opportunities has cost me, I have found in almost every situation that the situation got worse. If I had just done the dang thing when it needed to be done, I would have avoided a much bigger problem. If I could have just taken a step back, looked logically and objectively at it all, quieted the voices of worst-case scenario anxiety, and just remembered it was gonna be okay, I woulda been so much the better. I would certainly be at least $3,200 richer, but in reality, it's probably a lot more than that!

But here's the deal. Even with the hell I've had to pay for avoiding things I didn't want to do, *I'm still here.*

Even though my procrastination has caused everything to go to pot more times than I can count, sometimes in horrifically devastating ways, I'm still here. And honestly, the times I've failed miserably have given me a necessary humility (being humiliated has a way of doing that) and, if I may say so, a wisdom that having made all the right decisions could not have given.

Neither my procrastination nor the consequences of it are final.

No matter how badly I got it wrong, that is not my identity. I am not my procrastination. I am not the $3,200 I lost because of my stalling.

Those experiences don't define me, but they can refine me. They can make me a better version of myself. They can make me a better husband. A better dad. A better citizen. A better friend. Heck, even a better water-spigot fixer.

I now get to have the benefit and privilege of looking back on all those moments when I got it so wrong, and as much as they were gut-wrenching at the time and may have caused more than a little tension between Amanda and me (because what wife likes to hear that her husband's procrastination cost them the kitchen table they were hoping to get or the down payment on a house they were saving for), we actually just laugh now. Because we get to see how it all played out. Hindsight sure is twenty-twenty.

Somehow God always provided for us. Every. Single. Time. From the most random places we never would have seen coming. It has actually gotten to the point where when we get some unexpected check in the mail for something we had totally forgotten about, we wonder what is my next mess-up that God is preemptively providing for us and taking care of.

I don't think God's promised provision gives me permission to keep being an idiot. I really do try to learn from my mistakes and implement the lessons learned to avoid chaos in the future. I also don't think it permits me to foolishly rush into making decisions without thinking it through, which is sort of the antiprocrastination I am likely equally subject to be tempted by because of my personality. But I think it's just one more assurance that no matter what, no matter how badly I get it wrong, it's gonna be okay.

So if I know all this on the back end of the experience, what if I were to just start reminding myself at the beginning of the problem.

"Hey, bro! *[Yes, I call myself bro when I'm internally monologuing.]* I know you're worried. I know this is not gonna be fun, and it's probably gonna suck a lot. But you know what? It might not! It might not suck at all! It might only marginally suck but be over super quick. Either way, you're a grown man, and life isn't all fun and games, even for party animals like you. If you keep putting it off, it's just gonna suck more. So get off your patootie, put on your big boy boxer briefs, get it done, and remember it's gonna be okay."

Don't let your fear of the unknown keep you from acting in your own best interests and the best interests of those in your life. Your mind will play tricks on you. It'll inflate even the smallest mole hill into Kilimanjaro.

You'll subconsciously imagine that the pizza guy on the other end of the phone is actually a blood-sucking demon waiting to climb through the air waves to harvest your soul and turn you into some hollow shadow of a human, reminiscent of a scene out of *The Walking Dead*.

But in reality, he's just a sweet guy named Herbert, waiting to take your taste buds on a one-way trip to Pleasuretown with his cheesy, carby, culinary goodness.

LET'S BE REAL

Now, to be realistic, all your decisions to not put off till tomorrow what you need to do today may not have the same heavenly short-term consequences as ordering the dang pizza, but you still gotta do it.

That hard conversation you know you need to have may mean the necessary ending of a relationship you know isn't good for you. It may be lonely for a bit. You may feel misunderstood. It's work to find new friends. But the cancerous effect of bad company will no longer have its hold on you, and you'll be free to be the real you.

Talking with a counselor, pastor, trusted friend, or wise mentor to help heal from past pain may mean you have to face some things you don't want to deal with. It's gonna be hard work and probably take a good bit of time. Things like that are rarely fixed with Band-Aids and clichés.

Doing your taxes is literally the least fun thing on earth. But getting it done on time is far better than getting a letter in the mail telling you they're gonna freeze your assets because you didn't get it done.

I don't know what your thing is. But I know you have something. Because you're a human. Outside of the highly unlikely event you are artificial intelligence or a gorilla in a lab they taught to read, you are human. And all humans have *stuff*.

I don't know what you're walking through. But I know you're walking through something. Or maybe you just did. Or you're getting ready to. I've come to see that that is kind of the cycle of life. You're either in a storm or you're about to be. Of course, not all storms are created equal.

Yours may be heavy, or it may just be the inconvenience of a water leak or an overdue car registration, or even ordering a pizza over the phone.

But no matter what your situation or circumstance, call me an unempathetic realist if you like, but you have a choice in how you respond to it. And I believe you are gloriously free to grab the bull by the horns and own it like a boss. No matter how bad it seems, it's probably not as bad as you think, but it's definitely not as bad as it'll be if you let it simmer in its procrastinatory juices. Save yourself and everyone around you the heartache and headache. And the cash. It's gonna be okay.

Now if you'll excuse me, I've got an appointment at the vehicle registration office.

CHAPTER 5

THERE ARE NO SHORTCUTS!

S tephen?" my principal asked me from across his desk. This was a desk I had become all too familiar with from all my different mis-adventures, but this time, he had a little bit of a smirk like he was trying to hold back from laughing hysterically.

"Yes?" I said, half expecting his next words to be quoting Mr. Belding: "Remember the last three letters of *principal* spell 'pal,' and that's what I am . . . your pal!" This is not what came next.

"I had no idea you were so well-connected with such fascinating celebrities, Stephen! Tell me, how do you know Michael Jordan, Mike Tyson, Troy Aikman, MC Hammer, Michael Jackson, Wayne Gretzky, and Garth Brooks?"

I started sweating profusely. Despite my ardent admiration for each of them, I didn't truly know any of these people. Which meant my little ruse was up.

Rewind to the previous week when at a school assembly, a very nice mustachioed man in neatly ironed pleated Dockers and a slick cordu-roy blazer pitched my entire fourth-grade class on the virtue of selling Christmas wrapping paper. Table number one was covered in glitz and glam. Sparkling pink to tinsel red to green flannel. Every dazzling color of paper you could imagine in ten-foot rolls, just waiting to wrap what-ever my grandmother had thoughtfully picked out for me at the dollar store or thrift shop that year.

It was a fundraiser for something. We had no clue what. Could have been to help upgrade the sloppy joes in our cafeteria, for all I knew. Or to help them get some whole milk instead of having to get 2 percent. It didn't matter.

Because for the entire time the mustache twitched up and down over his lips with what I could only assume were words coming forth from his mouth, all I could focus on was the black blanket draped over table number two. That was the real reason for this assembly. To appeal to little boys' and girls' baser covetous instincts of greed and lust.

"I can see you kiddos aren't that interested in wrapping paper. You just wanna see what's under the blanket here, eh?" he said, in a halfway patronizing tone befitting a salesman of his Burt Reynoldsesque stature. Only if Burt Reynolds had somehow mastered the art of combining a thick Southern drawl with the speed of a Micro Machines auctioneer's speech. And then like a magician unveiling the final illusion, he whipped off the blanket with a voilà that had the kind of panache one might expect in a high-dollar Vegas show. The treasure trove he uncovered was mind-boggling.

Tiny little Dallas Cowboys helmets.

Silver sparkling slap bracelets.

Hacky Sacks that looked like they must have been made with the same materials as Joseph's coat of many colors.

Tootsie Roll piggy banks that were *full* of Tootsie Rolls!

That last one was the kicker. I muttered under my breath in a sort of *Wayne's World* "breaking the fourth wall" kind of way, "She will be mine. Oh yes. She will be mine."

I grabbed my fundraiser order form with lightning speed and ran home as fast as my chubby little legs could carry me. I took a shower, put on my best button-up shirt and khakis, wet my comb and slicked back my little chili bowl haircut to channel my inner Andy Garcia as much as possible, and even snuck into my dad's bathroom to borrow some of his cologne. I wanted to look professional. Like a real salesman. And since my mom was always going on and on about how handsome Andy Garcia was, I figured he was the guy to emulate if I was gonna get all the moms and grandmas on the block to purchase whatever wares I was peddling.

As I began going door-to-door in my neighborhood, little old lady after little old lady would tell me how excited she was to support me. "Put me down for a roll of wrapping paper," they said in the sweetest way possible. At the end of the day, I had sold fifteen rolls of wrapping paper, as well as two boxes of chocolate and one candle! Licking my lips, I opened up the rewards guide to see how many more I needed to sell to get the Tootsie Roll piggy bank. I was certain I was close, and I could taste those Tootsie Rolls already. Not to mention the massive amount of money I was gonna get to save after I plowed through all the candy and then began putting all my extra hard-earned cash in the bank. I was already visualizing all the incredible things I could buy after saving up for years in that thing.

But my heart sank a bit when I looked to the key next to the Tootsie Roll piggy bank and realized it required fifty points. I had only earned eighteen. If it took that much hustling just to get eighteen points, how on earth would I get another thirty-two?! Even if I asked all my relatives, that might procure me another ten, but I'd still be miles away.

It's like when you go to the arcade and you win like seven thousand tickets in Skee-Ball only to realize that the five-dollar Nerf gun you wanted is actually 1,225,000,012 tickets. That's how I felt. Didn't quite seem to add up. But I still needed to have that Tootsie Roll bank. And I was determined.

I racked my brain for days, trying to figure out how to make up the difference. All the other kids came into the school bragging about how their parents took their order forms to the office and sold to their coworkers for them and they already had a hundred points. They'd be getting the helmet and the Hacky Sack at least. I wasn't greedy! I just wanted the bank!

And it was at that very moment my imagination began to hatch a plan that was so completely perfect, so completely unique, so completely preposterous it had to work.

I reached for the order form as if under the inspiration of the great geniuses of olde, and it was like my pen was writing all by itself.

Line 22: Michael Jordan—4 rolls of wrapping paper

Line 23: Troy Aikman—3 rolls of wrapping paper

Line 24: John Smith (I needed to break up the famous names before it started to look suspicious)—1 roll

Line 25: Michael Jackson—1 box of chocolates, 1 candle, 1 roll of wrapping paper

Line 26: You get the point.

It was brilliant. Until it wasn't. I turned in my order form the next day, and my teacher was thrilled to see I had my fifty points. I stood there waiting for the piggy bank to be handed over, only to be informed that once the products came in and I was able to deliver them and collect the money, then I'd get the bank. That wasn't good.

So there I sat across from my principal, who, after graciously not reminding me that the last three letters of principal are "pal," was lovingly informing me that I wouldn't be getting the Tootsie Roll piggy bank unless all my celebrity "friends" had legitimately placed the orders and that one day after taking them their very real products, I would show up to school with a literal envelope containing $500 of non-*Monopoly* money from the sales I had made. I think he was halfway impressed, but he also had to be a "responsible" pal and let me know my shortcut wasn't going to work. I apologized and went home to tell my parents what had happened. Figured it was better coming from me than him. They laughed, and that was basically it. My shortcut hadn't worked, no matter how genius it was. It was still a shortcut, and shortcuts don't work.

SOME PEOPLE GOTTA LEARN
THE HARD WAY

Just a few short years later, I got caught up in another fundraising scandal. Some people just have to learn the hard way. I've been hearing the phrase "some people gotta learn the hard way" my whole life. My parents used to say it (probably referring to me), and it's in the opening line of an old DC Talk song that spoke to me a ton as I was growing up, partly because of how catchy the hook was, but more so because of how much I identify with it.

I had sold like a hundred chocolate bars for a dollar each, only to lose the envelope with the money. I panicked like Uncle Billy from *It's a Wonderful Life*. There was no way I could make up a hundred dollars! I was certain the sheriff and bank examiner were gonna show up at my house and carry me off. I was mortified!

Then it hit me. Like a light bulb going off in the Scarecrow's head.

We live in a capitalistic society. Supply and demand run the world. It's economics! Like how my gas was $2.65 yesterday and is $2.99 today. Next year it'll probably be like $4.50 a gallon. Crazy how that works.

I still had 150 bars left to sell. I would just sell the remaining bars for two dollars a pop and make up the difference I had lost! I stood out in front of Walmart like a nice little Girl Scout and off-loaded thirty there. Then on to the local hair salon across the street from my house, where I got another twenty-five sold. I was well on my way.

Until the next day, when I was called into the principal's office. "Hey, Stephen! Tell me, how are the chocolate bar sales going?"

"Really good, sir! People really love these things! They practically sell themselves!"

"Well, that's good! I can imagine they must, since you're selling them for two dollars when they are *clearly marked* one dollar."

I hadn't thought of this. There was a massive $1 on the packaging right next to "WORLD'S FINEST CHOCOLATE."

I mean, *world's finest* chocolate was a bit of a stretch and felt like false advertising to me. Kinda like the gas station that has a bright neon "World's Best Cup of Coffee" sign hanging in the window. Someone is telling a little white fib right there.

I mean, have you tried Chocolove Peppermint in Dark Chocolate? Now that's the world's finest chocolate right there, trailed only slightly by Lindt Lindor Dark Chocolate Truffles. But I think saying "World's Finest Chocolate" on the wrapper is still an easier stretch than selling a clearly marked one-dollar bar for two dollars.

"The ladies at the hair salon called up here to ask if they were supposed to be selling for the one dollar as marked or for two dollars because you're selling them for two," he said, continuing to press.

"Well, sir, I ran into a little snag. I actually had sold a hundred of them for the one dollar and somehow misplaced the money envelope, so I figured I could make it up by selling the rest for two dollars."

"Stephen, I'm actually impressed and quite amused here, but you're gonna have to return the extra dollar to the ladies at the salon and figure out a different way to make up the difference." I went to the salon that afternoon and handed back over the cash, I suppose just blindly trusting that the owner would find the ladies to give them back their hard-earned dollars.

Talk about taking the wind out of a young entrepreneur's sails! I ended up mowing five lawns for twenty dollars each and forked over all the money to cover my "World's Finest Screwup."

There are no shortcuts. You have to pay the piper one way or another. You've heard the phrase "work smarter, not harder." Well, as much as I like the idea of that, I think it's more like "work harder *and* smarter!" There really isn't a substitute for this!

A LITTLE HARD WORK . . .

But it's not like that's the end of the world. My parents used to tell me, "A little hard work never killed anybody." I don't know if that's true. I'm sure there are probably a few people who have died from working hard, but the point is, don't think you can just get to the top of Everest without doing the work. It's gonna be okay if you gotta pay some dues. It's okay if you have to get coffee for your jerk of a boss and say, "Yes, sir!" even when you don't agree. It's okay if you aren't making six figures in your first job and don't get promoted to CEO in your first week. And truthfully, it's quite possible you're gonna have to work a lot of jobs you hate before you get the one you love.

It's okay if you don't lose a hundred pounds after a month of working out and eating right. Sometimes things take time. And that's okay. Don't get discouraged. Just keep going. It's gonna be okay.

I've always struggled with my weight. From the time I was a kid, as far back as I can remember, I could look at a brownie and gain five pounds, smell it and gain ten, take a bite and gain twenty. I started to kinda obsess about it in middle school. My diet consisted exclusively of those Lean Cuisine frozen dinners and baked potatoes with "I Can't Believe It's Not Butter! Spray" because the old Fabio commercials just sold me on it. I can't say it without it being in Fabio's voice. Low fat. High carb. But it didn't work. I fought my weight until I hit more than three hundred pounds in high school, and, considering my five-foot, three-inch frame and the fact that I didn't really have a growth spurt until my senior year, this was problematic.

Then in 2001, I discovered the Atkins diet. It was carnivore heaven, population me. All the bacon and cheese my heart could desire, so long as I avoided carbs like middle school girls run from Axe body spray!

I managed a pizza shop at the time, so every day for lunch, I hand-made a triple pepperoni, triple cheese personal pizza with extra sauce and no bread. One thing you need to know about me is that I could eat pepperoni pizza every single day for the rest of my life and never get tired of it. So this was the easiest diet in all of existence.

Then upon my arrival home that evening, I would go about my master chef routine of pan searing my $2 shoulder steak to medium-rare perfection, complete with a can of green beans, which worked well on the $75/month grocery budget I was able to pull together out of the $1,100 I made each month running the pizza shop.

I lost a hundred pounds that year. Through a ton of crazy hard work and discipline. Two to three hours a day in the gym and not a single carb for a year.

However, eating that much fat day after day for years doesn't really repair your metabolism. There's only so much bacon and cheese a guy's arteries can take before they start to vehemently scream, *Whoa there, buddy! Let's not get too carried away!* It is, in essence, a quick-fix form of shortcut-taking that doesn't help much in the long run.

So after a few years of stress and busyness and dadding and job changes and travel and getting older, I started to put the weight back on. I would yo-yo twenty pounds here and there, then thirty, then forty. Then after we adopted Penny and Lincoln from China, with all the stress and sleepless nights and McDonald's because Penny was obsessed with "hambaobao" when she first came home, I just jumped all the way back up to 275. It was insane. The moment I stepped on the scale and saw the number, I was on a warpath. There was no way I was going back to the old me.

That week, I read an article that essentially said, "Coconut oil is great for weight loss." I interpreted this as though it were some sort of magic bullet I could use to show my man boobs who's boss. So while it said to just use a little bit, I threw caution to the wind and stacked up on the stuff—two tablespoons in my coffee first thing in the morning, two tablespoons in my second coffee two hours later, two tablespoons in my LaCroix at lunch. You get the drill. I was sure I would lose fifteen pounds that week if I just had enough coconut oil. The first swig I took, I felt a little like Dirty Harry and may have even said, "Well, fat, you gotta ask yourself one question: Do I feel lucky? Well, do ya, punk?" (Only my wife can testify to whether or not this is true, and she is sworn to secrecy.)

Turns out, it did feel lucky, and I spent twenty-three of the next twenty-four hours on the toilet, which feels a lot less like Clint Eastwood than how I pictured it going. Not to be graphic, but it destroyed me. I definitely lost weight, but it wasn't the kind of weight I wanted, and as soon as I ate anything, the weight was back.

As if trying this once wasn't enough, I did it a few times, all with the same results. My wife and kids actually started to make fun of me for how much I was in the restroom.

There are no shortcuts.

TRUST THE PROGRAM

The cost far outweighed the benefit of the coconut oil "approach" to weight loss, so I wised up and asked a coach to help me. I hired a trainer and nutritionist who has spent more than a year giving me the right tools to do the work to repair my metabolism and give me a healthier outlook on life, food, exercise, and more. I'm looking at my stress levels and how much sleep I'm getting and the other myriad factors that go into holistic health. It's more work than I've ever put into my health and has taken longer than I wanted, but week after week, I'm growing healthier in my late thirties than I've ever been in my entire life. Because I'm refusing quick fixes and working smarter and harder than I ever have, I'm setting myself up for the rest of my life.

One thing my coach said to me was, "This isn't a quick fix. It's gonna take a long time. But it's gonna be okay. Just trust me. Trust the program." You hear that? It's gonna be okay. These were the words my heart needed to hear. Even though it was gonna suck, it was gonna be okay. Not just okay, but far better than I could have imagined. I just had to put in the work and be patient.

He also told me I'd mess up and fall off the wagon from time to time. I'd have a cheat meal from time to time and go on vacation and eat like crap for a few days here and there. I'd miss workouts and lack the motivation to go as hard as I really should sometimes. But the key is not to let that one day of getting it wrong turn into a week that turns into a month that turns into a year of getting it wrong. When you mess up, it's okay. Get back up and get back going.

> Your failure isn't final. It's not who you are and it's not who you're becoming.

Essentially, he was giving me the three tenets of the epic fail in a way only a trainer and nutritionist can.

Your failure isn't final. Just because you screwed up and ate some ice cream or pizza or some glorious chips and queso doesn't mean it's over. Don't let this get you off the track. This isn't who you are, and it's not who you're becoming. So keep going.

I've lived basically four decades now, which is not a lot in the grand scheme of things. I feel younger than ever, and I keep hearing forty is the new thirty. But I'm also at the age where I'm just about as sure there are no shortcuts as that the sun will rise tomorrow.

No shortcuts. Not in work life. Not in family life. Not in spiritual growth or our favorite hobbies. Not in sports or music or art or science. As far as I know, shortcuts are just not a thing.

MY FIRST REAL SIX-STRING

When I first decided I wanted to learn to play the guitar, I borrowed a trashy twenty-dollar loaner with a neck so thick it could have doubled as a railroad tie. Then I locked myself in my tiny little bedroom of our duplex in Austin, Texas, and practiced for eight hours a day that entire summer until I could emerge, guitar in hand, playing with the confidence befitting a high school boy who had never had a girlfriend.

My fingers bled for three weeks as I woodshedded my way to proper calluses. My hand cramped incessantly until it got strong enough to handle the chord formations. Every cent I made from my job at Old Navy that didn't go to helping my mom with groceries went into saving up for my first guitar—an old pawn shop Ovation that could only be played standing up because its rounded back slid off my knee as quickly as I rested it there. It was a compromise to be sure, because what I really wanted was this sweet black Takamine G-Series for $549, which felt like a fortune to me as a kid of a single mom on a second-year teacher's salary.

Eventually I saved enough to negotiate a cash deal for $399 plus the Ovation trade-in. Feeling the fruit of more than a year and a half of practicing and working and saving fleshed out in a guitar neck that didn't feel like I was strangling a tree trunk is still one of the most satisfying sensations I can describe. It came at a cost. And it was absolutely worth it.

This is the guitar I wrote my first song for Amanda with. This is the guitar I used to record that song for our first Christmas together. This is the guitar I hid in the back of a horse-drawn carriage that passed by the Spaghetti Warehouse (where we'd had our first date) at "just the right time" for us to hop in and take a ride around downtown Austin, where I could pull it out from the back seat, sing the song to her, take out a ring, and ask her to be my wife forever. The hard work pays off, my friends.

About a year into our marriage, I started giving guitar lessons to supplement our income. With a baby at home, I had finally graduated from making $1,100 a month at the pizza shop, but I had also graduated to a lot more expenses. Diapers aren't cheap, y'all, and the six hundred boxes you get at your baby shower go fast. So after I finished up work at the rodeo arena I was managing (yes, you read that right), I would drive to students' homes and attempt to convince them that they actually had to practice if they wanted to learn anything from the guitar lessons I was giving them.

Turns out most people trying to learn how to play an instrument are just trying to take a shortcut to being able to play their favorite song. One particular student was a middle-aged man, who, while being one of the friendliest guys I've ever met to this day, was obsessed with learning to play "Wild World" by Cat Stevens. Each week, I would encourage him to practice, and each week he would say, "I know, man. But all I wanna play is Cat Stevens."

"Yes, I get that. It's gonna be okay, bro. We'll get there. But there are no shortcuts. You gotta learn the basics before we can move on to that. You can't run until you learn to walk." I would teach him the same dang thing every week, and then he would set his guitar on the stand in the corner, where it would stay until I came back the next week. He quit after four months, no closer to his goal but with about $700 less than he had when he started.

Fifteen years later, after having vowed to never teach guitar again, I finally convinced myself that I could take on a single student. A promising fourteen-year-old girl who was crazy about REO Speedwagon, Matthew West, and *The Greatest Showman*. The big difference was, when I taught Evelyn Grace a series of chords, she'd come back the following week having fully mastered it. After a month of practicing for hours a day, she was ready to learn a song. Then another. Then another. Until she could play in the school talent show, where she knocked everyone's socks off.

Anything worth doing will take work. And time (and, consequently, patience). And anything worth doing well will take even more work and time. But trust the process. It's gonna be okay. We all want to get where we're going quicker. And sometimes you can. But as a man who has gotten more speeding tickets than I care to divulge here, I don't recommend it. Haste, as they say, makes waste. When we try to shortcut the process, we are the ones who miss out. The journey builds our character. It strengthens us. It refines us and shapes our perspective on life, the world, ourselves, and everyone around us. It gives wisdom that only time can buy. It is the adventure. Or as Miley puts it, "It's the climb."[16]

A LONG WAY TO A DEAD END

You may need a guide or a game plan, or even an entire cheerleading squad's worth of encouragers, to help you make it to the finish line. You may need to stop for a breather or a glass of cold water along the way. You most certainly are gonna need a good kick in the pants, or 3,472 of them.

You're gonna want a few good Band-Aids and maybe a glass of Two Buck Chuck every here and there. You're gonna come across shortcuts your whole life. And you'll be tempted to take them.

My dad used to take shortcuts pretty much anytime we went anywhere. This was before phones told you where to go, and even before you could print out directions from MapQuest. Heck, this was before the internet was even in our house! My parents had folding maps and road atlases that helped them navigate to wherever we were going. But my dad rarely used them.

I'd hear my mom ask, "Where are we going?" from the front seat. He would reply, "We're taking the shortcut." Without fail, his shortcuts turned out to be the scenic route that took at least three times longer. This may have been his design all along. It gave him more time to finish a few more cigarettes. And with the windows down and the wind in our hair, it gave us all more time to sing along with Crosby, Stills & Nash as we gazed out onto the Oklahoma countryside. But a few times his shortcuts took us to a dead end. We would have to turn around and go back the way we came.

The shortcut somehow, more often than not, ends up being the long way to a dead end. And that's okay. At least you got the scenery and the extra time with your music and the wind in your hair. And you have some fun stories to tell later on. It's not the end of the road if you slip up and mistakenly try the shortcut, whether intentionally, stubbornly, ignorantly, pridefully, or because you got bamboozled. We all get bamboozled sometimes. It sucks when that happens, but life goes on. That's part of the art of getting it wrong.

You'll survive your shortcuts and live to play another day, hopefully a little wiser and a little humbler than you were before. And that's never a bad thing.

CHAPTER 6

WATCH YOUR BLIND SPOTS

I could feel the power in my fingertips as I gripped the leather steering wheel. My heart pounded with excitement as I lowered my foot onto the gas pedal and listened to the massive engine roar like the beast it was. Amanda and the boys giggled from the back seat as I grunted like a caveman, giddy with anticipation of the test drive I was getting ready to embark on.

Two miles later, we circled back, and I sat in a small corner office shaking the firm grip of a gentleman wearing a three-piece suit who had some of the most enviable sideburns I'd ever seen and a power tie that could go toe-to-toe with any Fortune 500 CEO. I was buying the Hulk of all trucks. A forest green Ford Super Duty F-250 King Ranch. Lesser men may have needed a stepladder to get in, but not me. We had been eyeballing this thing for years in hopes that one day we could pull a dream wagon behind it and tour the nation with our gigantic family. Worldschooling at its finest. We didn't choose the RV life; the RV life chose us.

Our imaginations were running wild as we played out every possible scenario in specific detail. Teaching the kids math at the Grand Canyon. American history in Philadelphia, Boston, and New York. PE class hiking in Yosemite. The Green Beast was our ticket to adventure. And we were finally there.

We left the dealership and did what every hot-blooded carnivorous man in my situation would do. We drove three miles down the road to The Salt Lick BBQ (google it and be prepared to wipe the drool from your mouth) and gorged ourselves on every tasty morsel of exquisitely crafted brisket perfection our bodies could possibly handle before the meat sweats overtook us and put us in a coma. Though I'm fairly certain my son Liam ate twice as much as me (oh, to have his metabolism), I have never felt more like a man.

That was the best truck I have ever owned. And I have owned two, so that's saying something.

The next day, Amanda took our son Lincoln to his new physical and occupational therapist. I hadn't had the privilege of coming to a session yet, so we made plans to meet up there and go grab some coffee afterward. I was so eager to see the progress he was making after his brain surgery and could hardly wait to get in there and watch them working with him!

If you're unfamiliar, we have a six-year-old son who has pretty severe special needs after having several strokes as a baby caused by a rare brain disease called moyamoya. He has left-sided hemiplegia, a form of cerebral palsy that has made it exceedingly difficult to learn to walk and use the left side of his body, while also severely limiting his development and speech.

And yet by the grace of God and an absolute ton of therapy each week, he has experienced miracle after miracle. He's now walking when they said he never would and starting to speak in some ways as well! We know we have a long way ahead of us, but these therapies and therapists have been so amazing to watch, and on this particular day, I was rushing because I was so excited to see how he was progressing!

I turned under the intersection to what I assumed was a green light based on how traffic flow usually goes, but I was looking past the intersection ahead, searching for the turn into the therapy parking lot when I felt a little jolt. Enough to move me a bit, but not too jarring. Until I looked out my passenger window and saw a Mustang butted up against my wheel!

I rushed to open the door, dropped the twenty-two feet to the ground from my driver's seat, and ran the hundred yards around the front of the Hulk to check on the other driver, a girl in her early twenties who stood there surveying the situation in disbelief. (Okay, I promised not to exaggerate. It was probably only four feet from the driver's seat to the ground and about ten yards around the front of the truck.)

The Green Beast appeared to have survived without a scratch, but that gorgeous Mustang was gonna need some work in the body shop. Either way, she was probably gonna get to drive around a sick minivan rental for a few days while it was getting worked on. #Winning.

As we were able to establish that no one was hurt, we all began to loosen up and started to joke around about how much this sucked in the most reassuring way possible, given the situation. I mentioned in the previous chapters that I've been told every once in a while that I'm not especially self-aware. And in most cases I would adamantly disagree with the accusation, but in this particular situation, as I laughingly looked at her and asked, "Did you just not see the light?" I sure wished that the Ghost of Christmas Self-Awareness Future could have paid me a visit with a little gift of foresight. My proverbial rose-colored glasses were suddenly proving not so charming.

Three quasi-jovial onlookers' demeanor changed faster than you can say, "I got ninety-nine problems, but a truck ain't one," and began to charge at me like ravenous wolves with wild "how dare you!" looks in their eyes, screaming in frequencies I imagine only dogs could hear.

"You Were the One Who Ran the Light!"

I was completely taken aback—there was no way this was my fault. I had just turned under the intersection to a light that was green. But one by one, witness after witness tore into me, saying they had just watched me coast on through the red light and the Mustang couldn't stop in time to avoid hitting me. I looked back at one guy who was particularly silent, waiting for some backup here, when he shrugged and said, "Sorry, dude. I was right behind you, and you ran the light."

Was I in *The Twilight Zone*?

The police and fire department arrived on scene, and as they walked up, one of the cops muttered into his radio, "Yeah, the usual spot." I asked him to clarify what exactly he meant by "the usual spot."

"Well, we have about five wrecks a week here because they have the timing on the lights off right now. Everyone goes under the intersection thinking the light will be green, so they aren't paying attention and just run the red. We've reported it as a major problem, but they're taking their sweet time getting it fixed."

Are. You. Freaking. Kidding. Me?

I was shaking. Furious. Heartbroken. Bewildered. How could I have possibly been so blind? Regardless of whether the light's timing was off or not, I wasn't paying attention the way I should have been. I was responsible. I should have noticed the light was red. I should have stopped. I shouldn't have been in the middle of the intersection.

Ten minutes ago, I was headed to see my son trying to learn to walk. Now I'm stranded in this intersection with a girl who's gonna be stuck in a Dodge Caravan for a week while her baby gets fixed. The weight of the realization of my fault hit me like a ton of bricks, and I could hardly take it.

Just as I started to feel like I couldn't hold back the tears anymore, Amanda rushed to assure me with her merciful arms wrapped securely around me. I had been so embarrassed that I didn't even see her get to the scene. But she just held me right through it. She didn't scream or point fingers, though she could have. She didn't shame me or make me feel more like the failure I felt I was. She just held me and said, "It's gonna be okay." Somehow she knew that in that moment, those were the only words I needed to hear.

They towed the truck away, and we got a call that it was totaled. Turns out the Mustang hit the axle at just the right place to crack it. Who would have guessed? No more Green Beast. No more world-schooling at Rocky Mountain National Park. Luckily, insurance paid out enough for me to pay cash for an itsy-bitsy, teeny-weeny, no AC, black Jeep Liberty that overheated every single one of Texas's one hundred days of 100+ degree weather that year. I think I dropped twenty pounds in sweat alone. It was like my own personal sauna on wheels.

All because I was so caught up in the "what's next" that I couldn't see the "here and now."

We didn't vlog this. We didn't put it on the gram with a sob story to get sympathy or judgment or a mixture of both blended together like an expertly crafted cocktail from a newbie mixologist three months into quarantine. We just let life be life and allowed the embarrassment to subside. But now that a couple of years have passed, hindsight has taught me a few things.

As much as I felt like this wreck was the end of the world and life was over as I knew it, it wasn't. Life went on. Sure, my insurance went through the roof, but this failure wasn't final. I got a new mobile sauna I could drive around town out of the deal, and in just a few short years, my insurance will go down again.

No matter how badly I got it wrong that day, that's not who I am. Two years in, and aside from when I have to pay my car insurance bill, I think about it maybe once every couple months. Amanda doesn't bring it up or hold it over my head. She's just as gracious as she was on that first day. The kids have never even mentioned it. Even my in-laws have said

> Failure doesn't define me, but it is refining me.

next to nothing in a good thirty-five months, and even then, it was just trying to help us find a new vehicle. I'm not my mess-up.

That failure doesn't define me, but it is refining me. I'm learning to pay attention and keep my eyes on the moment right in front of me.

Watch your blind spots.

DISTRACTED BY TOMORROW

We all have blind spots. Whether they're caused by our personality, past trauma, pride, defensiveness, infatuation, or just plain ignorance. This world is full of millions of things that have the potential to skew our vision and distract us. For me, it's usually dreaming and driving toward the possibilities that tomorrow holds.

I have been a citizen of Tomorrowland for as long as I can remember. The problem with this is that it blinds you to the beauty of *today*. And like me eagerly anticipating the next turn and missing the red light right in front of me, that can put you in quite the predicament. Maybe it's not a Mustang that totals your new truck. Maybe it's missing the most precious moments of your kids' lives because you're too caught up in worrying about what's just over the horizon. Maybe it's a relationship that shrivels up on the vine because you were too preoccupied with your future hopes to nourish the now. It's entirely too easy to let the grass in your yard become a brown and brittle fire hazard because your eyes are dead set on the other side of the fence, where the green grass taunts you, keeping you from seeing what's right in front of you.

For me, a big blind spot has been trying to prove I actually matter because I didn't believe I did. I spent decades working to reverse the childhood wounds of bullying, rejection, poverty, and abandonment that I somehow internalized to mean I was worthless. As a result, I've spent way too many hours being present without being *present* than I would care to admit. In my mind I was home and therefore available, but in reality, Amanda and the kids got the top of my head more often than the dignity of my eyes. I would be immersed in some planning session or off in dreamland. Never really looking at the intersections right in front of me, always with my eyes on that upcoming turn toward some fantastic, gloriously enviable life that would "show them."

Early on in our marriage, that blind spot played itself out in an obsession with becoming a famous rock star. After a long day at the rodeo arena, if I wasn't playing in a club, I was tirelessly researching venues I could send my music to so I could book that next gig. I was convinced if I could play enough shows and get in front of enough people, my band would somehow become the next big thing and people would finally see I was worth something.

Reese was a baby, and her curiously cute little self was starting to be more mobile and experiment with developing her panache for, shall we say, "unique" ways of getting my attention. We called her a bit of a Houdini because she was always getting into some mischief and had more than a few surprises up her sleeve.

One evening, as I sat there on the computer carefully composing an email to try to book a particular gig in Houston that had been on my hit list for quite some time, I was a little too distracted to realize I had more intergluteal cleft peeking out of my pants than a plumber on a full moon. Reese definitely noticed it. And as she had been trying to get my attention for the last thirty minutes so I would drop work for just a bit and play with her, she was ready to disrupt my preoccupation with future fame.

Amanda watched with equal parts horror and hilarity as Reese studied the crevice protruding from my pant line and, as if in slow motion, reached her fingers directly into the fault line. I jumped up immediately, abruptly shocked out of my future-fame-induced trance. Then as quickly as the terror came on, it subsided and was replaced with irrepressible laughter.

"I think someone wants you to play with her," Amanda laughed. She knew all too well how it felt to try to get my attention, and I think she was sort of applauding Reese's brilliant approach to obtaining it. Thankfully, neither of them, nor anyone else for that matter, has ever repeated this particular tactic.

Amanda knows my past and my wounds. She knows the baggage I carry and actively fight against. And I'm so grateful that she loves me enough to gently call out the blind spots they cause in my heart. Sometimes it catches me off guard with a jolt and it feels a lot like that intersection twilight zone where I'm like, "No way did I run the red light. I'm just working to provide for my family."

Sometimes it really is just that my personality has always been the driven-dreamer type—a sort of mixture of P. T. Barnum and Ferris Bueller. I'm what's known as an Enneagram Type 7w8. For those of you who aren't familiar with this personality type, I'm basically the guy who is always up for that next adventure and doesn't know how to sit still because I can't stop thinking about whatever comes next. I wanna do it all, see it all, taste it all, have it all, and go go go go go until it's all been done. And apparently this is because I was wounded at a young age and vowed never to feel that way again, so rather than feeling sad, I minimize my pain with happy thoughts and daydreaming. Sounds familiar.

SONGS IN THE KEY OF ME

I was so honored when Ryan O'Neal (a.k.a. Sleeping at Last) wrote a song all about me. I have never had anyone do that other than Taylor Swift's "Hey Stephen." And while Taylor (yes, we're on a first-name basis) was right that I look like an angel, I think Ryan summed me up a bit better with his *Atlas: Enneagram* song "Seven," which he could probably have just called "Hey Stephen, Part 2." But since he doesn't even know who I am and doesn't realize he wrote it about me, I'll give him grace here.

After brilliantly and poetically diagnosing me with witty line after witty line, showcasing my propensity to not be able to sit still while making long lists of all the amazing things I want to see and do and accomplish, no matter how much it costs the people who love me, the progression of the song shows someone growing in maturity. Learning that they have enough. Learning to care about the people right in front of them. Learning to *truly be here*, before launching into its climactic summary of its soaring last chorus: "Restless and hungry, I'm ready for whatever comes next."[17]

As if to say, this is always gonna be something you struggle with, but at least you know, so you can fight well!

The hurt in my past has shaped me in ways I am still learning about and will be discovering for years to come. The restless hunger for what's next. The insatiable need for adventure. The temptation to ignore my pain and act like everything is just fine. The gravitational pull to prioritize experiences over relationships. They say your greatest strength is usually your greatest weakness too. I think that's probably the case with my personality. As much as my personality has made life happy and fun, adventurous and exciting, for me and my family and friends, it has also created the most fertile soil for blind spots to grow in my easily distractible heart.

I'm no expert on the Enneagram, and I have some reservations about letting a personality profile determine who I am and how I think and feel, but what I do know is that over the last few years, I've really been challenged to take a deep look at my unhealed wounds and trauma and deal with it. Stop minimizing the hurt or pretending it's not there. Stop stuffing it down or ignoring it or acting like everything is just fine.

Really, truly examine the wounds and address them. Because they aren't an excuse to go out and run red lights and wreck people's lives.

PRESENT AND COMPLETELY LOVED

I don't know that I'll ever not be a dreamer. I don't know that I will lose the entrepreneurial desire to build and create and innovate. But I do know that as far as it depends on me, I'm going to do everything in my power to keep what matters most in the forefront of my perspective. To keep the main things the main things. To remember that I don't have anything to prove and that I am already completely loved despite all the craziness in my heart.

I don't want Amanda and the kids to know the back of my phone better than my face or the rat race of social media to be the mistress home-wrecker that robs my family and friends of the real me. Maybe you can relate.

The reality is it's gonna be okay if I miss out on a good thing because I am prioritizing a great thing.

It's gonna be okay if I miss out on a few opportunities because I refused to miss out on being present with my family.

It's gonna be okay if I don't make quite as much money next month because I chose to make memories with my wife and kids instead.

I'm learning that I will never regret choosing to slow down and check my blind spots before making decisions. It's gonna be okay if I don't get there as quickly. Heck, it's gonna be okay if I don't ever "get there" because here is a pretty great place to be right now, when you consider the alternative of, well, not being here. Even if *here* is a tough place and you're walking through the thick of it, *now* is still the only place you can actually get anything done, unless you've figured out the secret of time travel (and if you have, please travel back to 2007 and tell me to buy a bunch of Netflix stock).

Jesus was incredibly smart when he said, "Do not worry about tomorrow, for tomorrow will worry about itself."[18] Tomorrow is quite literally a blind spot. It's pointless to be anxious about it. You have no idea what's gonna come into your life and what's gonna leave. You have no control over that. And you don't need to.

That doesn't mean you don't plan and work and pray and dream. Dream big! Bigger than you ever thought possible. And have a blast doing it! But don't let tomorrow's dreams blind you to the tangible joys of what's right in front of you right now.

Breathe deep. Bask in the sun and enjoy the breeze on your face. Savor your food. Dance in the kitchen. Look people in the eye. Smile ginormously. Laugh hysterically. Take naps.

Be present. Intentionally present. Gloriously present. Uncomfortably present. Irrationally present. Take care of today, and I promise you, tomorrow is gonna be okay.

CHAPTER 7

THE BONE CRUSHER

M ILLER!"

I didn't move. Didn't even notice my name being called.

"MILLER! You! Come on!"

I looked up sheepishly at J. D., a popular, athletic eighth-grade boy who was handpicked by our way-too-short-shorts–wearing, whistle-happy, Crocodile Dundee–looking PE teacher to be captain of the maroon team for that particular day's indoor soccer festivities. He was motioning me over. I was stunned. My name had been called *first*.

Not only had I never been picked *first* in my life, but this momentous occasion marked the singular anomaly when I was not picked *last* for any and every sport.

To be fair, I'm not altogether what most people would call "athletic." Never have had that particular gifting. So as a general rule, I would stand against the wall, waiting longingly for someone to call my name, and without fail, every time I was left alone, anticipating the loud groans from whatever team ended up getting stuck with me. I was just deadweight no one wanted.

But not this time. That day, J. D. saw me as an asset. As a strength to the team. "I bet you can kick pretty hard, Miller. Let's win this thing!" he said in a way that made me believe him. I wasn't last picked; I was first. I can't remember a single name of the rest of the kids in that class. But I'll never forget J. D.

Growing up as the fat kid didn't *just* mean I was the last pick in every sport. It didn't *just* mean getting friend zoned by every girl I ever liked. It also meant I was bullied pretty much nonstop and got into a lot of fights. Like, almost every day. I even threw a kid through the wall at church camp once. And while I've never had a broken bone of my own, a few of those fights ended in the other kid having a broken arm, leg, or nose. But that's not what got me the nickname Bone Crusher. No, that came from my best friend, on whom I happened to have a major crush for years, constantly trying to figure out how to get her to forget about my other best friend, with whom she had been head over heels in love since they were babies. I couldn't blame her. He was a star athlete and musician who surfed and snowboarded and had six-pack abs to complement his signature shaggy blond hair that all the girls were crazy about.

I had a six-pack too, I would try to tell her; it was just hiding in the fridge.

For the better part of my sophomore and junior years of high school, we were dang near inseparable. We went to the same church youth group, and every Wednesday night and Sunday night we would all go out and eat at Taco Bell or Culver's or go play Putt-Putt or bowl or something or other. Pretty much any excuse to hang out.

One particular evening, I thought it would be funny to flirt a little (kids, don't try this at home) by grabbing her keys and taking her car for a leisurely spin in the parking lot. There were only two problems with this idea: the first was that I didn't have a driver's license; the second was that she was on the hood of the car when I hit the gas. For some reason, my little teenage-boy brain envisioned I would just freak her out a little and then park the car so we could hug it out—major bonus—and have a good laugh. This was sure to endear me to her and help her see we were destined to be together forever.

Instead, I turned the car a little too abruptly, and she slid off the hood and fell to the ground with a single bounce and a loud crack upon impact with the concrete parking lot.

Crap! I had broken her arm. Well, technically, the pavement had broken her arm. But I was definitely the cause of the misfortune.

Two things happened in that moment:

1. I invented a new way to *not* flirt with a girl to add to my ever-growing list.
2. My new nickname was born. *Bone Crusher.* It just kinda stuck, and honestly, I didn't mind. It had a nice ring to it. Certainly better than a lot of the other nicknames I've had in my life. My kids call me Stevo now, which is nowhere near as cool. I have tried to tell them it reminds me of a greasy-haired frat boy who hasn't showered in weeks and thinks a funny prank is sticking butt lint in someone's water when they're not looking. Maybe I'll have them start calling me Bone Crusher again. That'll get me the respect I deserve.

Needless to say, I never got the girl. And that's okay. She married her betrothed from birth and they have four amazing kids now. We are still good friends, and they will still call me Bone Crusher from time to time, though usually they just call me Stephen Miller. (Never just Stephen. Always *Stephen Miller.* Still, it's better than Stevo.)

SOMEONE WHO SEES THE REAL YOU

I once took a girl to a winter formal dance who left with my sister's date. The next year, I took a girl who took that opportunity to let me know she already had a boyfriend and was really sorry she had been leading me on for the last six months. High school is brutal, and for me rejection was kinda just part of the deal.

I wish I could go back to my fifteen-to-seventeen-year-old self and tell him it's gonna be okay. Because this whole feeling of being rejected yet again pretty much crushed me to the point that I swore off girls completely. This was just the latest in a lifelong line of girls for whom I wasn't skinny enough or cool enough or popular enough or charming enough.

My mom could tell I was in a funk. Her usual jovial, glass-half-full joker of a son was clearly jacked up. Night after night, she would hug me and say, "It's gonna be okay. Someday you're gonna meet a girl who will see the real you and love you for you. I promise you. It's gonna be okay."

I would roll my eyes skeptically and say, "Yeah right. You have to say that because you're my mom. That's never gonna happen."

And yet just a few short months later, there I was, daring to daydream and night dream and mid-morning dream and every-other-part-of-the-day dream about a breathtakingly gorgeous, angelic blonde named Amanda.

I was crazy about Amanda Nagel from the moment I walked into the cafeteria and saw her sitting across the room in her white sweater, glowing like an angel. She was surrounded by boys who were all in love with her, and no matter what she was saying, they were laughing hysterically. Band nerds. Football stars. Shaggy-haired drummers. Artsy-fartsy rich kids. Khaki-wearing preppies. Macho men who hunted and fished and made their own beef jerky. They all adored her. They thought she was a righteous dudette. And I could see exactly why.

I knew she was so far out of my league that I didn't stand a chance, but by this time, I was a senior and had learned to be a bit of a clown and disarm people with silliness, so I was gonna give it my best shot. This girl was worth taking a chance on. And if she wasn't interested, I could play it off like I was just being a nice dork.

I motioned to my bass player, Matt, who had been sitting with her, and asked, "Dude, who is *that*?"

"Oh, that's Amanda Nagel. She's our keyboard player at church!"

"Holy hell! She plays keys? Gaaahhh! She looks heavenly. I'm gonna go talk to her."

I walked right over, plopped down next to her with a boomingly loud thud and, about as awkwardly as I think is humanly possible, said, "Hey, I'm Stephen!"

She didn't know what to make of it, but hesitantly responded, "Oh . . . hi . . . I'm . . . Amanda."

I switched to that lunch hour to be able to sit next to her every day from then on. For months, I chased her down and wore her down until she agreed to go to prom with me for our first date. She looked more stunningly breathtaking than anything I had ever seen, and we did some of the most epic hand-holding in all of hand-holding history. I'm certain that never before and never since have two individuals held hands with such zealous fervency. It was clumsy and weird and awkward and perfect. We still talk about it to this day.

But the next day, I let my fear get the best of me. I just didn't know what to do with all those feelings, and I didn't want to let my heart get shattered yet again. In an effort to protect myself against the imminent rejection I saw coming, I sat down with her and had *the talk*.

"Listen, I really like you, and I think you like me too. But I'm going off to college soon, and I don't want to do a long-distance relationship."

She looked bewildered. "Okaaaay."

"I think we should just be friends."

Who the heck was I? The friend zonee had become the friend zoner! Bone Crusher, indeed. She played it cool and hugged me as we parted ways. But that night as I lay in bed, I couldn't get the nagging voice out of my head that shouted at me, *You fool, what have you done? You freaking idiot!*

That next weekend, April 30, 2001, I was banking on the Founder's Day celebration in Dripping Springs, Texas, being about the only thing to do in our tiny hometown. This meant Amanda would be there and I could ask her to be my girlfriend officially. I asked my mom if I could borrow the car, and I drove downtown, frantically searching from street to street until I caught sight of Amanda's streaming strands of golden hair and piercing emerald-green eyes from blocks away. Call it having a knack for the dramatic or just being a hormonal teen boy, but I was fighting back tears as I parked and rushed to get her attention.

> I'm an idiot. I don't even know what I was thinking. Will you go out with me? Check yes or no . . .

Luckily for me and our seven kids, she opted in to receive my messages and we have been texting ever since.

At this juncture, I feel it's important for you to know that as I wrote this, I just spontaneously burst out into the chorus of Garth Brooks's "Unanswered Prayers." I wasn't kidding when I said I'm a die-hard Garth fan. So I'll do that from time to time. It can be weird for people who don't know me, and most of the time, no one in proximity has ever heard the song 'cause I can go for those deep cut B-sides sometimes, making the chances of anyone jumping in to belt it out with me on the chorus slim to none.

If you're unfamiliar, the song recounts the tale of a guy who is minding his own business at a local high school football game when he runs into a girl he used to be in love with back in the day. He had prayed every night back then, begging God to make her fall in love with him so they could be together.

Long story short, the experience was sorta jarring. When he looks over to see his wife standing there, he's overwhelmed with gratitude for his prayer not being answered after all, realizing God knew *exactly* what he was doing the whole time.

BETTER IS OUT THERE FOR YOU

In this life, you're going to deal with heartbreak and rejection. It sucks, but it's gonna happen. Maybe it's not about getting the girl. Maybe it's feeling passed over for the raise or promotion, wondering why everyone else seems to get the breaks you've been longing for or even genuinely need. Maybe you feel like the last one picked or the one forgotten by the people who were supposed to choose you first, whether it's a friend or a partner or a parent. Those feelings are very real and very gut-wrenching. If I could somehow magically or miraculously save you from having to experience them, I would. But I can't.

> Tears and pain may be blinding, but tears are not wasted and they're not forever.

All I can do is do what my momma did for me. Tell you it's gonna be okay. And mean it. Because it's true. You may not see it now. The tears and pain may be blinding. But tears are not wasted, and they're not forever. One day, you're gonna wake up and have that moment when you realize that something far better was waiting for you than whatever you were pining over.

That's not to say it will be an easy road to get there. It may take some significant work to become the person you need to be to receive whatever the better thing is.

If you're out there bone-crushing people to try to get their attention, you may need to rethink your approach. If you really are a greasy-haired frat boy who puts butt lint in people's water as a prank when they're not looking, you should probably cut it out.

It may involve learning how to talk to a girl in ways that don't make them hate all men, and vice versa. Or developing the job skills to get that promotion you need. Everyone has to pay their dues sometimes. If you're dreaming of marrying some tall, dark, and handsome Spanish heartthrob, you may have to learn Spanish.

You may need to raise your standards and stop letting the person who's supposed to love you the most walk all over you. You're not a doormat, and no one is so great that they can treat people like they don't matter.

We should all be constantly evolving. Learning. Growing. Maturing. Improving. Becoming.

But even still, with all of that, you can only control what you can control. People are people everywhere you go, and sometimes they just won't see how gloriously *you* you really are because they can't see past how gloriously awesome *they think they are.* And as much as that will hurt in the moment, you just gotta know that better is out there for you. Don't shut down your heart to self-protect, and don't insulate yourself to avoid getting hurt in the future. The biggest problem with shutting down your heart to avoid pain is that you also miss out on the joy and beauty that is out there for you to delight in every single day.

It may not look how you think it's gonna look. The prayers you're praying may be answered in ways you never saw coming, and it may look like silence, like "unanswered prayers." But I believe in a God who actually knows what he's doing, and he's a lot wiser, stronger, and more loving than I could ever imagine. He knows what I actually need. He knows when I actually need it. And he knows the best medium for me to receive it.

I actually trust him with this. And when I start feeling my trust in him begin to waver, I just think back to that day in the cafeteria when the Bone Crusher met his match.

The pain of today will give way to the beauty of tomorrow. The torrential downpour will make the valleys verdant. The struggle up the mountain will give you the best views over all the places where all the tears were worth it.

CHAPTER 8

LIFE MOVES PRETTY FAST, AND IF YOU DON'T STOP AND LOOK AROUND, YOU COULD MISS IT!

If you haven't already picked up on this yet, I'm a walking encyclopedia of pop culture, movie quotes, and song lyrics, particularly from the 1980s and '90s. Maybe it's because there were no iPhones or iPads and really not even the internet yet. Social media was just a glimmer in Tom Anderson and Mark Zuckerberg's angsty teen eyes.

The closest thing we had to YouTube or podcasts was carrying around the Talkboy 24-7, trying to capture the sound of our teachers farting in the hallways.

So rather than quoting old Vines and practicing TikTok dances, my eyes were glued to our little wooden-encased, turn-dial TV and VCR. *Ninja Turtles*, *A League of Their Own*, *Braveheart*, *The Sandlot*, *The Princess Bride*, and *Billy Madison* were my babysitters. So even to this day, if you spend more than twenty minutes with me, you'll probably hear a quote from one of these classics. Whether it's "There's no crying in baseball!"[19] or "I could crush you like a worm."[20] or "Shampoo is better!"[21]

It's become a running theme on our vlogs because of the sheer joy I get when someone recognizes some obscure quote and calls it out with appreciation! Like there is a disproportionately massive level of happiness that wells up in my heart when someone comments, "That's from *Killer Klowns from Outer Space*!" There are very few sentences that come from my mouth that aren't at least influenced by '80s and '90s movies.

Of all of them, I think the one that rings most true to my life comes from the brilliant wisdom of *Ferris Bueller's Day Off*: "Life moves pretty fast. If you don't stop and look around once in a while, you could miss it."[22]

MEASURE TWICE, CUT ONCE

As an Undiagnosed, but Self-Professed Specializer in ADHD Activity and Behavior (or USPSADHDAB for short), I can often end up making a mess of things because I get carried away going too fast and end up missing something.

Outside of my wife, my father-in-law probably has more stories to testify to this fact than anyone else on the planet. In so many ways, he taught me what it means to be a man. How to change my oil and change a tire. How to make a sale and negotiate a contract. When he hired me to manage the rodeo arena at twenty years old, I had no clue how to do anything. But there was plenty to do.

He taught me how to drive a forklift and a tractor. How to take care of horses and muck stalls. How to build stuff and fix stuff—from broken pipes to framing and drywalling. Over and over, I heard his calm voice: "Stephen, don't force it. Stephen, slow down. Careful." But the one I remember most is, "Measure twice, cut once." The idea is to double-check your work and you'll have a lot less waste as the result of your haste.

He started telling me this shortly after he let me borrow his Black Beauty diesel engine Ford F-250 to drive his daughter to Galveston for our honeymoon cruise. We may have been the most excited little newlyweds the world had ever seen, but we didn't exactly have a reliable truck to drive a few hours away to the port, so he let us use his with the warning, "Make good choices," as we took the keys. Of course, I had the best intentions to make good choices. After all, I was getting to travel the Caribbean with the most beautiful woman on earth who was now my wife! What could go wrong?

We started to get low on gas as we approached the halfway point, and I pulled into the gas station—in quite a hurry to get there. Rushing to fill the tank as quickly as possible, I picked up the fuel nozzle, shoved it into the receptacle on the truck, and let the gas begin to flow, when about halfway through, I realized the folly of my ways.

This is a diesel engine.

I'm putting regular gas in it.

I shut the pump off, worried out of my mind that not only was I going to miss my honeymoon, but it was going to be because I turned this Black Beauty into a one-ton bomb just above a reservoir of fuel big enough to destroy ten square blocks! I had seen *Zoolander* way too many times to not picture the extreme devastation of the film's gasoline fight playing out vividly in my mind. I was freaking out.

And also super embarrassed. How was I gonna tell my father-in-law that I probably ruined his truck? But what other choice did I have? I pulled my sweet Nokia 3310 phone out of my pocket and dialed his number by memory. Sweet, sweet man. I was his first son-in-law, and I was gonna send him to an early grave from worrying about how his second of four daughters was gonna survive my stupidity.

He patiently talked me through how to switch over to the other fuel tank (the truck had two tanks, thankfully) and under no circumstances ever switch it back to this one unless I wanted to explode. I think the only words I was able to get out were, "Yes, sir."

ACROSS THE POND

Ten years later, Amanda and I went on the most epic of all adventures for our tenth wedding anniversary! We had been saving like crazy and found the most incredible deal on Groupon for eleven days in London, Paris, and Rome. Flights and trains included. Hop-on hop-off tours in every city. Hotels and breakfast. You name it. All for $1,000 a person. We couldn't pass this up.

Our hotel was just off Gloucester Road, pronounced Gloster but definitely *not* Glochester, as was kindly explained by a street cop the first time I asked where the Gloucester Road tube station was, with a very pronounced *ch* sound unwelcomingly stuck in the middle. From the "Gloster" Road station, we raced in a tube underneath the streets of London for three days. Cruised up and down the River Thames. Big Ben. London Bridge. Tower of London. 221B Baker Street. Fish and chips. Piccadilly Circus. St. Paul's Cathedral.

I spoke in a British accent the entire time, and the only time I was ever "caught" was when I tried to order a coffee at the Starbucks next to Buckingham Palace.

"What kind of coffee?" the barista inquired.

"Just a coffee . . ."

"Yeah, but what kind of coffee?"

"Just a normal coffee. With a little cream." I started to get a little flustered. "Like a drip coffee."

"Oh, an Americano. Got it."

Who would have known my great obsession with caffeinated goodness would be the downfall of my greater obsession with English accents. I had spent a lifetime perfecting it, and a cup of coffee ruined it all.

At the end of our three days in London, we traveled to the St Pancras railway station to make our way to Paris. In my excitement to see the city I had dreamed of my whole life, I had been rushing around to see it all and do it all so much that I had hardly looked at the train ticket to see what time we departed. So it was a bit of a shock when we arrived to check in and were informed that our train had left for Paris hours earlier. I'm still not exactly sure how it happened, but I was under the impression we were leaving in the early evening, when in fact our train had taken off that morning.

They could still get us to Paris that day, but it was gonna be another few hours and another $700 to make it happen! Luckily, we had $1,000 in our emergency fund and were able to pull the trigger, but that one hurt. I still wish I had slowed down long enough to "measure twice, cut once" on the departure time and save myself the frustration and the money. But we did find the silver lining as we held hands in a nearby romantic café and found out that Platform 9 ¾ at King's Cross Station was right across the street. One last bucket list item. And we still got to sleep in Paris that night.

For whatever reason, no matter how many opportunities I get, I don't seem to get the lesson through my head until I have to learn it the hard way. You would think that $700 would be a painful enough way to learn how to slow down and pay attention a little. But you would be wrong.

MY LAST-EVER SPEEDING TICKET

Just a few months after returning home from London, Paris, and Rome with my bride, who I failed to mention was four months pregnant, I was scheduled to teach at a conference in Austin, Texas, for what *should* have been two weeks after our son Ethan was born. Amanda was born and raised in Austin, and her entire family was there. So for us, living in St. Louis, this felt like a great opportunity for the family to get to meet our new son! And beyond that, this was a conference I had wanted to be part of for a while and I was extremely honored to have been asked to teach at it.

So after Ethan's due date came and went, we began to get a little anxious for his arrival into this world. Not just because Amanda was more than a week late and ready to be done being pregnant. Not just because we were so overwhelmingly eager to meet our son. But we were also worried that if he didn't hurry up and get here, we were gonna miss the conference and our chance to visit our family back home!

Amanda tried massage and chiropractic treatments. We did castor oil and spicy food. We took long walks and drove on bumpy roads. We did basically everything you can do to try to induce labor. And none of it worked. We were starting to worry.

But finally the day arrived, and Ethan made his appearance on his own schedule and in his own time, which he has been doing ever since. I held that little baby boy in my arms, and there in the hospital room, we watched the St. Louis Cardinals face down the Boston Red Sox in the World Series, whispering in his ear, "This is our game, buddy!" It was a type of euphoria I can hardly describe, but it made me forget how anxious I was that I was supposed to be in Austin the next day to teach at the conference.

After being discharged from the hospital, picking up the kids, and packing our bags, we hit the road at 5:00 a.m. the next morning with the Lone Star State in our GPS and the Show Me State in our rearview. If I played my cards right and made everyone pee in a cup instead of stopping (I'm exaggerating here, and since I promised not to exaggerate in this book, I would like to clarify that I would never have actually made my beautiful bride and mother of my newborn son pee in a cup), we would still make it in time for me to teach that night.

I may have been a little too gung ho, because the next thing I knew there were red and blue lights flashing behind me and a Ray-Ban-wearing Erik Estrada look-alike motioning to me to pull off the highway.

I pulled out my driver's license and insurance card and held them out the window with my other hand on the steering wheel as the kids looked on in amazement. I didn't have time to argue. My plan was to just shut up and let him write the ticket so we could be on our way.

"Do you know how fast you were going?"

"Pretty sure it was maybe 85?"

"No, sir. Try 92."

"I'm very sorry, sir."

He took what felt like three hundred years to write my ticket, and as he handed it to me, I thought to myself, *I'll just pay this later and get on with it. How bad could it be?*

We made it to the conference, and for a few moments, I was thinking it may have been worth it to have driven so recklessly and that while the haste had made waste, it would probably only be about $300 of waste and that's not nearly as bad as $700 for the train, so I would actually come out ahead here. Until I returned home and called the court to pay the ticket.

"Hello, ma'am, this is Stephen Miller. I got a ticket a week ago, and I'd like to pay it . . ."

"Sorry, sir, you can't just pay this ticket. It was more than twenty over the speed limit. You have to come in for your court date."

I lived hours away from this little town in Oklahoma and wasn't too jazzed about the idea, so I asked my lawyer neighbor, whom I had affectionately named Fun Bobby after, when slightly inebriated, he smashed his hand into a strawberry cake Amanda had made for my thirtieth birthday and proceeded to eat it before anyone else could get a bite. He always had a surprise up his sleeve, and if anyone could get me out of this, it was Fun Bobby.

But after assuring me he could, he then did some research and realized it was, in fact, a nonstarter. I would have to go to court for this *minor* infraction. My only hope was that the cop wouldn't show.

I rehearsed my lines over and over on the few hours' drive to the courthouse. I would plead guilty, sincerely looking the judge in the eyes and telling him how truly repentant I was, and ask for mercy. I had grown up in the church, and if this was good enough for Jesus, it would have to be good enough for this guy, right?

Having a last name that started with *m* put me at the end of a very long list of people ahead of me for their hearings. Which meant I got to see how this thing worked. How the judge treated each case. How the lawyers interacted with him. The judge seemed lenient and logical.

He called a man to the platform for grand arson and resisting arrest and let him off with community service and a $500 fine.

The next man was given community service and a $600 fine for assault with a deadly weapon.

I felt like I was in the clear and started to breathe easier.

Until a sixteen-year-old girl with the last name Landers walked up to the platform and a Ray-Banless Estrada stood up as well. The judge began to speak.

"Miss Landers, you're here for going 91 miles an hour in a 70 miles an hour zone. Officer, what are you going for here?"

The officer said, "I'd like to go for jail time. Thirty days. This girl has gotta learn."

The judge looked at the girl and said, "I see you don't have a lawyer here. Would you like to delay this hearing until you can get a lawyer?"

I'm not sure if she peed her pants, but I sure just about did. If this was how they were treating a young girl who had never had a speeding ticket, I was done for.

She walked off the platform and left the building to fight another day just as they called out "Miller! Stephen Miller!"

I stood up and the same play unfolded. I declined to delay the hearing due to my lack of representation and immediately launched into my speech.

"I plead guilty, Your Honor."

"Wait, wait, wait, wait!" the judge interrupted. "Now hold off. Are you sure you wanna plead guilty to this? You don't wanna get a lawyer? You know the officer here wants to put you in jail!"

"Yes, sir, I understand that," I replied, "but I can't afford a lawyer and I am guilty. I was speeding when I shouldn't have been. I was in a hurry and didn't stop to think of the dangerous ramifications of what would happen if something went wrong. I am truly repentant and asking for mercy. I have a newborn at home and it would be very difficult on my wife if I had to spend thirty days in jail while she looked after our five children."

"Mercy, eh? You want mercy? I'll tell you what I want. I want your kids to have a dad. I want your kids to not have to get a letter or a phone call that their dad died because he was going too fast. So we are gonna put your repentance to the test. I'm gonna put you on two years of probation. That's two years. 365 days times two. And if you get so much as a single speeding ticket in that two years, I'll know you weren't truly repentant and you're gonna be sitting in my jail for thirty days. How about that?"

> Mess-ups and mistakes should get you to slow the heck down.

I walked out, paid my court fines, registered with my probation officer, and drove home grateful I wasn't headed to jail. And you know what? I haven't gotten a speeding ticket since.

It would be easy to let those moments haunt me rather than teach me. It would be easy to complain about having gotten a raw deal rather than accepting the responsibility and letting it change me into a better version of myself.

The truth is, no matter how badly I got it wrong, my failures weren't final. I'm not my speeding ticket or my train ticket or any other ticket. I'm not my horribly executed British accent coffee order or the misspoken *ch* in *Gloster*. My failure doesn't define me, but it can refine me. And it is. My mess-ups and mistakes are shaping me to slow the heck down. Yours can do the same.

SLOW THE HECK DOWN AND JUST BE

Life is crazy and awesome and wonderful and wild, and I believe God has a way of giving us chances to learn how to slow the heck down and not miss it. When you don't learn the lessons he is patiently trying to teach you, sometimes he'll escalate the stakes a little. Whether it's a full tank of unleaded gas in a diesel engine, an unexpected $700 at a train station, or two years of checking in with a probation officer, subtle and not so subtle reminders are all around us, echoing the words of Ferris Bueller.

Every breath we have is a gift. Every moment is a blessing. And the hustle and bustle and busyness of life are constantly trying to rush you through those miraculous moments that are pregnant with awe and wonder. Whether it's the birth of your son or daughter or the aroma of romance and fresh bread baking at a train station boulangerie.

I don't know what you need to do to help you build margin into your life so you can slow down and breathe. I don't know what will help you measure twice so you only have to cut once. Maybe it's putting thirty minutes or an hour between meetings. Or getting up thirty minutes earlier so you don't have to rush to get ready to make it to your workplace on time.

One of the greatest habits I've started cultivating in my life this past year is building four one-minute pauses into my day. I use that minute to offer up everything I'm doing to God in a prayer. To give him all my worries and work. To give him anything I'm anxious about or feeling stress over. My opportunities and plans, my marriage and money. I set an alarm, and as soon as I hear it, I drop everything and force myself to slow down and just *be*.

Not do. Not strive. Just be still.

When you're hurried, you miss out on the beauty surrounding you.

When you're hurried, you miss details that could be the difference between having to completely start over and finishing early. (If you've ever tried to put together IKEA furniture, you know what I'm talking about.)

When you're hurried, you hurt people. It's practically impossible to be kind to the people around you when you see them as obstacles to getting to where you want to be.

When you're hurried, it almost always just ends up getting you nowhere faster and costing you more to get there.

That's not to say that life is over as you know it. It's still gonna be okay. If you gotta learn the hard way, at least you've still finally learned. Maybe not fully, but at least enough for now! Don't worry, you'll get another opportunity. And you may even get to visit Platform 9 ¾ in the meantime.

You may miss out on some pretty amazing things today, but that's the beauty of the sunrise. You get a new day tomorrow to slow down and drink deeply of the goodness surrounding you then. Isn't that great news?

The Bible says that God's mercies are new every morning.[23] And that's really good news for hardheaded, hurried people like me. I believe God gives me a new chance every day to still my hassled heart, seize the day, and suck the proverbial marrow out of life. He gives me the adventure of seeing that the people in my life are gifts and that the journey is just as beautiful as the destination.

This past year, I made the alarm I wake up to every morning the nostalgic, gravelly voice of Louis Armstrong singing, "What a Wonderful World." Those are the first words I hear every day. The slow, flowing whole notes of the strings subtly coax me to pace myself and remind myself to "see" the wonder of every moment. It's my favorite song of all time, and it's slowly shaping my hurried heart.

Life moves pretty fast. But it's gonna be okay if you don't move fast with it. Slow down. Stop and look around. Don't miss it.

CHAPTER 9

TURNS OUT, YOU CAN GET CHIANTI PRETTY MUCH ANYWHERE!

Sometimes the best order to go in is chronological. Of course, social media forgot about this a long time ago, giving us algorithms that show us whatever they want. I hate this because I feel like I probably miss a lot, but this approach isn't always a bad thing. Sometimes chronological is boring. Doing things out of order can often make things more interesting.

Like watching *Lost* with its myriad flashbacks that add texture and character development layer after layer. Or *Tenet*, where you don't exactly know what timeline you're in, and you're not really sure if you ever will, but it's the not knowing that ties it all together in a sort of satisfyingly mind-bending feast of überintellectual science fiction!

I kinda like when movies or shows or books don't play by the rules, because my free-spirited, "come with me and you'll be in a world of pure imagination" self doesn't like to play by the rules either.[24] This approach has taught me that everything is gonna be okay the hard (but worthwhile) way—one epic fail at a time.

So as I've gone back and forth with my publisher about the chapter order for this book, we have given a lot of thought to whether these stories need to be in chronological order. And for the most part, I think we've landed on keeping it more like thematic popcorn on the lessons I've learned from the stupid stuff I've done. But in this particular case, I think it's best to return to a story from the last chapter—in Paris.

So close your eyes and picture this.

There we were, on the train pulling into the Gare du Nord, two kids wildly in love on our tenth wedding anniversary adventure, $700 poorer than a mere few hours earlier, but bright-eyed and bushy-tailed nonetheless. I half expected to step off the train to the set of *Hugo* but was instead greeted by a poster of *The Hangover 3* in French, and no clue on earth how to get to our hotel. Thank God for Google Translate and a decent grasp of Latin-based languages.

We finally found the hotel and proceeded to do the one thing every single food blog told us we had to do in Paris. Eat butter. Copious amounts of it. Any moment we could get our hands on it. We ate what I would estimate to be about forty-two pounds of butter in those three days. Pretty much anything we could get our hands on was just a vehicle for that deliciously creamy goodness to transport us into ecstasy yet again.

We danced in the courtyard of the Louvre, had coffee and crepes by the Seine, drank wine on the lawn of the Eiffel Tower, ate the most exquisitely perfect ice cream in existence from Berthillon as we toured Notre Dame Cathedral, shopped the Champs-Élysées while photo-bombing the Arc de Triomphe. We saw every square inch of the City of Love and City of Lights from a hop-on-hop-off tour bus. The architecture. The beauty. The romance. The history. All of this, and still the *butter* is the thing that left its eternal mark branded on our souls more than anything else. The food bloggers were right. They always are.

So making our way to Rome about twenty-two pounds heavier than three days earlier (speaking for myself—Amanda was eating for two, very pregnant with our fifth child, Ethan, who devoured all that butter from the womb without Amanda gaining a pound), we weren't sure we could ever love a city more than Paris. And especially since our entire taxi ride to the hotel just inside the Vatican walls was shrouded by the black clouds of a torrential downpour that blinded us from seeing anything outside of the rain curtains flooding our windows.

We practically dove from the car into the hotel lobby in a way that would have made James Bond proud, suitcases in hand, and made our way through the halls to our room as the rain continued to pound the hotel. I couldn't help but think to myself, *Please, God, don't let this be our whole time in Rome!*

Our flight to Italy that morning had been at 5:00 a.m., meaning we had to be there by 3:30 a.m., meaning we had to be up at 2:30 a.m. For a guy like me who requires maybe forty-five minutes of sleep a day, this isn't a problem. But for a woman who prefers to have nine hours when she's *not* pregnant, you can imagine my wife, who was single-handedly producing all the energy for two entire human beings, needed a nap.

I tried to lie down next to her so that our first experiences in Rome would be together, but my mind was racing. As a history fanatic, I was in the ultimate place. I wanted to see it all. Do it all. Taste all the things. Take all the pics! I didn't wanna be cooped up in a hotel, and my FOMO was starting to kick in.

So as Amanda's breath became steady and slowed, I whispered a prayer. *God, make the rain stop . . . like . . . now?*

God must have heard the trembling in my soft-voiced supplications because at that very moment—I kid you not—the rain stopped. I felt like Elijah. I crept out of bed with the stealth of a ninja and slipped on my shoes and then opened and shut our hotel room door as quietly as I knew how to just go "take a peek" at the streets outside our hotel. What happened next was like Dorothy waking up in Oz.

The doors opened from inside the dark hotel lobby to sunshine pouring down on my face, the wind blowing through my hair, the sound of accordion music playing (literally, real accordion music played by real accordion players). Street vendors were opening up their espresso shops on every corner. I strolled over and ordered a double cappuccino, and it is to this day the greatest coffee I've ever had.

People were singing in the streets at the top of their lungs. Not just weirdos like me who sing at the top of my lungs all the time. *Everyone* was singing. And dancing. And laughing. I started to wonder if this was *actually* my home. Like, I'm what people in Hollywood might call "ethnically ambiguous." I look like I could be Turkish or Mexican or basically from anywhere. Maybe I was actually Italian after all! Or maybe I was actually still in the bed back in the hotel room and had drifted off to sleep and was dreaming this utopia I was experiencing.

I rushed back to the hotel room to, first and foremost, make sure I wasn't still lying next to Amanda and, second, to wake her sleepy, little pregnant booty up so she could come see! We sucked the marrow out of life those next couple days, tired bones and all.

We were staying in the Vatican, so our first stop was to walk a block over to tour St. Peter's Basilica. Then we jumped onto our hop-on-hop-off bus to see the Colosseum, the Fontana di Trevi, the Pantheon, and the Roman Forum and to eat at all the restaurants but *definitely not* order the lasagna or pizza because that's what tourists do and we weren't tourists. We were honorary Italians for three days. On our last night, before getting some of the most insane gelato on the planet (I don't even like gelato, but this stuff will blow your mind—it's the real deal), we read up on a particular restaurant down the street from our hotel and just knew we needed to try it.

OUR LAST NIGHT IN ROME

We walked in, and the moment we sat down, the owner came out and greeted us with the kind of warmth you would expect from your long-lost benevolent grandpa you hadn't seen in decades, but it didn't matter because *you were home*! We couldn't decide what to order but had heard that the trick is to ask the servers what they are most proud of and let them choose for you. So I did! They began to bring out every imaginable appetizer, entrée, pasta, seafood—you name it—that I had never heard of, and every bite was the best bite I had ever taken!

A waiter walked by with a particular drink that looked good, and I asked, "What are they having to drink?" and then they brought us not only the white sangria I had inquired about, but also one of every drink on and off the menu with the kind of proud smile that said, "This one is the best drink . . . No, *this* is the best drink . . . No, *this one* is the best drink! *No, this is the best drink! No, this one is the best drink!*" You get the idea.

It was magical. I began to wonder if they were fattening us up for the kill. Perhaps they could smell the twenty-two pounds of butter pulsing through my veins. But even more important, what on earth was this gonna cost? I had only $300 left in my emergency fund. But when the time came for the bill, the owner simply walked up to our table, singing, of course, and said it was on the house. I tried to leave a tip, but he said their entire waitstaff was salaried and they don't accept tips. So I bought three bottles of their best Chianti for my father-in-law instead to support these people who had made this the best night of our lives so far! I knew nothing about wine and still don't, but Amanda's dad had talked about Chianti more than anything I could remember, except for making good choices, measuring twice and cutting once, and things of that nature. I figured I could score some brownie points and kill two birds with one stone.

You know how sometimes you think you're being detail-oriented but you're just not seeing all the details? Yeah, that's what happened to me. Problems arose the next day as we were going through security at the airport to fly home and give said bottles of life-changing Chianti to my father-in-law, who would henceforth deem me worthy of his daughter's love once and for all.

I was beyond certain that if I packed the Chianti bottles in my suitcase, some careless airport luggage loader was gonna chuck it as hard as he possibly could against the runway, thereby shattering all three bottles of my "favorite son-in-law" serum. So in what I thought was a brilliant move, I took out everything I'd normally put in my carry-on, shoved it into my suitcase, checked the bag, and proceeded to jam some pretty large bottles of wine into my backpack. What could possibly go wrong?

Airport security—that's what.

"Sir, you can't carry bottles of wine onto the plane," the security officer said in the kindest Italian accent. Some accents don't sound kind. Some sound harsh and angry. Some make you want to pee your pants. But not Italian. This guy was dropping some hard truth on me, but it felt kinda like a compliment. It's amazing what a killer accent can do.

"Oh, I'm sorry. I didn't realize I couldn't bring wine back home. This is for my father-in-law. Anything we can do about this? It's kinda my ticket to being loved as the favorite son-in-law for the rest of my life. So it's pretty important."

"It's not about the wine. It's that they're each like sixteen times bigger than the regulation number of ounces of liquid you can carry on a plane."

"Oooooooohhhhh . . ." It was starting to sink in.

"So you have two options. You can throw them away or you can give them to us and make two airport security employees very happy."

We chose the latter, and the smiles on those guards' faces are still etched in my mind to this day. I'm guessing you deal with a lot of disgruntled travelers in that line of work, especially if you're having to tell them to throw away precious cargo, so something like this made their day.

BRAIN FARTS AND BLESSINGS

Sometimes it's the inconvenient or even infuriating setbacks we come across that are actually the best opportunities to be a blessing to someone. Sometimes those setbacks are the direct result of our lack of attention to detail or brain farts that kept us from thinking things through properly. And those can be so frustrating in the moment, because it often means you're gonna miss out on something you were really looking forward to or wanting. But it's gonna be okay!

Turns out, you can get Chianti pretty much anywhere! A few years later, I found that exact bottle we had tried to bring home at a grocery store in Texas (thank you, H-E-B!) and was able to give it to my father-in-law for his birthday after all! And while I had already well-earned my place in his heart as the greatest son-in-law of all time by this point, I have rarely gotten to repeat chances to bless people who may need it in the exact moment of my most frustrating mistakes.

I miss this more than I get it right. But I'm growing and I'm learning. I'm trying to anyway!

On a different wedding anniversary trip—our eighteenth to be precise—we went to Zion National Park. We were staying in an Airbnb about forty-five minutes away from the park, and there was only one restaurant around. After repeatedly calling to try to place a to-go order and finding that no one answered, I decided to drive there and do it in person.

The hostess was very kind and attentive. A young college girl who seemed to be pretty new there, but you could tell she was trying really hard. I put in my order and was told it would be about an hour-long wait, so I drove back to our Airbnb and waited with Amanda.

When I got back to the restaurant, I waited another forty-five minutes before anyone even acknowledged my existence, and while I was doing my best to pass the time with YouTube videos of hiking Angels Landing, I could feel myself getting frustrated and considered just abandoning the order altogether. But I had already paid for it and was pretty much starving after a day of hiking with very little food.

Just then, two older couples, probably in their eighties, walked in, dressed to the nines. Two men in expertly pressed suits and ties, shoes shined, and smiles as big as the sky. Their wives on their arms, one in a red dress, the other in black-and-white polka dot, both in high heels, perfectly curled hair, and bright red lipstick. You could tell they were looking forward to this evening and probably had been for quite some time!

The hostess was coming off a break and saw them walking up to the stand. It was kinda hard for me not to be annoyed that she had seen them but not me, the guy who had been standing there waiting patiently for the last forty-five minutes. But then again, I was wearing workout clothes and they had basically stepped off the cover of *GQ*. One definitely captures the attention more quickly than the other.

As they approached, they gave their names with the sweetest, "Table for four—it's our anniversaries!" It was maybe the cutest thing I'd ever seen. But as the hostess looked over her roster of reservations, I could see her visibly begin to perspire.

"I'm so sorry, but it appears you all booked next Wednesday, not tonight."

The portly, balding gentleman on the right calmly took a step forward and respectfully removed his ever so fashionable fedora as he reached into his jacket pocket to pull out a reservation card that showed that exact time on that exact night.

"No, ma'am, it was for tonight."

The hostess began to panic, as did the trainer who approached the stand to help.

"I'm so sorry, we just don't have any room tonight. We have a wedding party that is taking up the entire restaurant. We actually closed an hour ago for the party."

I expected an uproar. Their plans were ruined. The anniversary dinner that they had been planning for and clearly spent more than just a little bit of time and attention to detail to make the evening special was a no-go.

Instead, I was shocked, surprised, and challenged in the most profound, unexpected ways. Instead of outrage, a gentle, soothing voice began to encourage her like a loving grandfather.

"Young lady, you are wonderful and beautiful, and we know you are working hard. This mistake could have happened to anyone. You can only play the cards you're dealt, and this dinner tonight just wasn't in the cards for us. We'll be back next Wednesday and are looking forward to it. See you then?"

He smiled at her, patted her on the shoulder, and turning to his three comrades with a wink, he held out his arm for his wife to take, and they walked out with more class than I have ever seen in four human beings.

I turned to the hostess and saw the tears welling up in her eyes. The kind of tears that seem to imply that maybe she had felt seen for the first time. The kind of tears that showed she felt like she had value and worth in the way you rarely get to feel from other people. That moment changed her day, and maybe her life.

I know it changed mine.

"I've never seen anything like that. What an amazing group of people!" I said.

She looked up at me, as if seeing me for the first time, and said, "Neither have I. I'm gonna cry. Oh my goodness, your food! We closed right after you left, and the kitchen still hasn't made it! I am so sorry! It'll be right out!"

Of course the bar was now set. I couldn't be frustrated at this point! I had just seen what may have been angels in disguise take their frustrating setback that was the result, not of their own actions, but of someone else's, and react with nothing but compassionate grace and patient kindness.

> We won't be like that at eighty if we aren't like that now.

I called Amanda to tell her the story while I waited for our dinner to be prepared. "That's how I want us to be when we are eighty."

"Well, we probably won't be like that at eighty if we aren't like that now, so we should probably start working on that today." We laughed. My wife is so perceptive and wise. And I have told that story countless times since.

MAKE SOMEONE'S DAY

How do I, how do you, how do we begin to look our setbacks in the face and not only tell ourselves it's gonna be okay, but take it a step further and say, *How can I be a blessing in the midst of this?*

Our setbacks are not always the result of our failures or of our getting it wrong. But that doesn't mean we can't learn from them. They aren't final. They don't define us. But they can refine us.

Maybe the setback didn't happen *to* you; it happened *for* you. Or for someone else!

Maybe those moments that are so frustrating, whether caused by our own hands or the hands of others, are just opportunities to make someone's day. To change people's worlds and to change our own.

There's power in that. And that's the kind of power I want. To be that guy, not just in my eighties, but here and now.

CHAPTER 10

THAT TIME I ALMOST DIED *AGAIN*!

have a knack for almost dying. I don't know how else to put it. I've had more close calls than I think any man deserves. I would say I'm like a cat with nine lives, but I think I've well overshot my nine-life allotment.

When I told my wife I was going to write a chapter about all the times I've almost died, she said, "Wow, that's gonna be a loooooong chapter."

You may want to sit down for this one if you aren't already. Maybe get a comfy little hammock or something.

In an effort to be transparent, I have entrusted my fact-checker-in-chief (a.k.a. Amanda) with the task of making sure I hold true to my promise not to exaggerate the facts of any of these stories. You can rest easy knowing that every single word is accurate and told to the best of my remembrance.

When I was in third grade, I had saved long and hard from mowing yards and finally had enough money to buy my first bike. I had been eyeing a Huffy on the shelves at Walmart for a little over a year, and every time I pulled on that mower crank, I could see myself jumping curbs and trying new tricks to impress the neighborhood girls. In my head, I was already a kung fu master, practicing against imaginary enemies in the front yard day after day with the moves I'd learned from the Ninja Turtles, Jean-Claude Van Damme, Steven Seagal, and Bruce Lee—all my personal mentors. I would throw on my Wranglers and my rugby shirt and go to town, moving from cartwheel and somersault to kicking the air as high as I could. But these skills never quite seemed to impress the ladies. So surely if I had a Huffy, it'd be all I needed to get them to notice me for more than a good laugh.

There was an old woman a few blocks down on the corner who was a constant source of revenue for me. But beyond that, encouragement. She had a little pug dog, and they would sit on the front porch together and watch me mow from the spring through the fall. She kept a box of orange creamsicles in her freezer for just such occasions, which she would break in half, giving one side to me and feeding the other to her little pug. When there was nothing to mow, she would ask if I could rake leaves. I think she liked the company as much as a tidy yard. When I told her one day that I had finally saved the $125 for the bike I had been wanting, she was overjoyed for me.

"Well, let's just hope you find something else to save for so you can keep coming back to help me with my yard," she said with a laugh as she handed me half of an orange creamsicle.

When I returned the next week, more than just a little bummed because my family needed my bike money to help with the groceries and I was starting again at square one, she didn't bat an eye.

"Stephen, you've been doing such a great job. But I think that today you did an *extra* good job. So I'm gonna pay you a little *extra*!" she said as she reached into her little snap purse, pulled out a little bit of folded cash, and counted out six $20 bills before handing it to me.

"How much did you say the bike was? I think that should cover it." I was dumbfounded. This was six times more than my usual rate, minus the creamsicle. "You go get that bike today."

I gave her a huge hug, overjoyed with tears in my eyes, and ran home to tell my mom, who took me to Walmart later that day to retrieve my prize. Finally! I had a bike! Of course, I would continue my training to be a ninja master of the highest order. But this would give me that extra edge.

We got home, and I immediately put on my helmet and walked my bike to the very top of the hill near where we lived. In third grade it seemed like a mile high, with a steady sixty-degree slope down to the bottom where our little rental house was. As an adventure seeker from the start, I was in for a hard-earned thrill. I started down the hill, pedaling as fast as possible to get up as much speed as I could, when at the bottom of the hill my mom stepped out and yelled for me to slow down and come in to eat dinner. Of course, I didn't know about centrifugal force, inertia, or even brakes for that matter. I turned left as fast as I could and before I could slow down even a little, my front tire collided with the curb, sending me flying over the handlebars and landing

There's always a silver lining.

directly on my knees, which skidded across the concrete sidewalk for a good ten feet, leaving my skin and about a pint of blood in my wake.

I was in pain, but my biggest concern really began to sink in as I looked at my bike's front wheel, which was bent into a sort of warbly, potato chip–looking thing. My first day with a bike, and I had already ruined it. But at least I was alive. And I had some war scars to show for it, which I had heard was a good way to impress girls too. There's always a silver lining.

CHARLES IN CHARGE

Fast-forward about nine near-death experiences and ten years later. Amanda and I had just gotten back to her parents' house after a lunch date on a blazing hot Texas Saturday afternoon. After trying the locked door, I remembered they always hid a key underneath a porcelain frog in a hutch on the far right side of the front porch. Just as I lifted the frog and reached to grab the key, I felt a sharp sting on my hand and pulled back as quickly as I could to see a yellow jacket come raging out of the hutch. There's a vein on the back of the hand that, for me, sticks out a little more when I'm hot, and that little bugger got me right on the vein. It *hurt*, but as far as I could tell, I was gonna be okay. So I retrieved the key, unlocked the door, grabbed a drink of water, and walked out to the barn to see if Amanda's dad needed any help with the horses.

Before I could even get a word in, Charles said, "Stephen, are you okay?"

He looked at me with a very concerned "what in the name of all things that are good and holy?" kind of way that started to worry me a bit.

"Of course! Why? I mean, I just got stung by a yellow jacket, but I feel okay. Why are you asking? Well, I guess my heart *is* racing a little bit and kinda feels like it's beating hard in my head. But I feel okay."

"Well, Stephen, you're sorta turning purple and shriveling up with hives. Have you ever been stung by a yellow jacket before?"

"Not that I know of."

He rushed me into the house, filled a tub with cold water and ice, gave me some Benadryl, and called the doctor. After I'd spent about an hour freezing to death in an ice bath, the purpleness, swelling, and hives went down and my heart rate slowed. It was gonna be okay. I was gonna need to get an EpiPen, because apparently if you're allergic to yellow jackets, it doesn't get better with time. If you're deathly allergic, you're deathly allergic. And I learned something new that day: I'm deathly allergic! But at least I had a superhot nurse to help me get back to health. No, not Amanda's dad—his daughter!

Amanda sat by my side, holding my hand the whole time while the Benadryl wore off and I finally woke up. There's always a silver lining.

I don't recommend getting stung by a yellow jacket to get a girl's attention any more than I'd recommend doing kung fu in the front yard or wrecking your new bike. It doesn't matter how good you are at using your dad's table saw blade as a ninja throwing star or how high you fly over the handlebars when you hit the curb. It would take a very special person for either of those to actually work. But there is something about a near-death experience that has a way of fusing two souls together, and I definitely fell more in love with that girl that day.

A couple years later, my nurse's dad hired me to run the rodeo arena he was contracted to turn things around at. It had been losing like $100K a year for as long as everyone could remember and needed some changes. For a job I hated every second of for three years, I sure do have a lot of fun stories from that place. One thing was constant— every week was different.

One week, we'd host a fair, and I'd come in and have to clean up all the places where the carnival workers had decided to go number two on the ground because they couldn't get into the bathrooms overnight.

Other weeks, I'd be cleaning up regurgitated menudo from week-long Cinco de Mayo raves where people got so drunk they couldn't hold down their stew. Then, as quickly as humanly possible, we would immediately have to find a way to make the place not smell like vomit because we were hours away from a cutting horse event where $1 million–plus horse trailers would pull in with some of the wealthiest, most successful horsepeople out there, and they weren't too fond of the uniquely pungent aroma of menudo vomit.

We held concerts, goat sales, horse shows, livestock shows, dog shows (I never realized how accurate *Best in Show* was until this job), barrel races, car auctions, biker gang rallies, and, yes, even rodeos.

Working at such a multifaceted events center meant we had to transform the property a lot. One day, we'd have 120 horse stalls set up; the next, we'd have them all removed and the arena steamrolled and rubber mats placed down for people to walk comfortably throughout the building.

I learned to drive a tractor and, what's more, a forklift. And I used them both *a lot*. But when your facility hasn't turned a profit in more than twenty years, they don't exactly have the money for state-of-the-art equipment. So while my father-in-law had worked a deal to have a local company donate a brand-new tractor, our forklift remained a dinosaur from a bygone era—a mustard yellow 1960s Ford tank that weighed nearly two tons. The benefit of a forklift of this magnitude was that it could lift a lot of weight, and we pushed it to the limits every week.

At one point, we had booked two fairly large events back-to-back and were in a crunch to transform the arena as quickly as possible. I had a gig that evening with my band and needed to leave early, so I decided to go to work a few hours early and start tearing down horse stalls. Our process was fairly simple:

1. Pop out the pins that held together each of the pure steel, 10-foot, 200-pound panels.
2. Slowly lower the panels onto the fork extensions, stacking them fifteen high.
3. Hop on the forklift and cart the panels to the columns against the perimeter fence about a hundred feet away.
4. Hop off the forklift and stack a wooden block on each of the four corners of the column of panels underneath.
5. Hop back on the forklift and align the extensions with the wood blocks.
6. Lower the stack of fifteen panels until it rests on the column and blocks.
7. Back up and repeat steps one to six until all 120 stalls are completely torn down.

The work is fairly rigorous, and you'd typically have a partner help you knock it out safely. But since I was in a hurry, I foolishly chose to knock it out by myself to get ahead of schedule. Only one problem. On this particular day, a (shall we say) "situation" arose right around step four. My 3,500-pound, mega-old forklift with its 3,000-pound payload decided to shift out of park and into neutral, just as I was stacking the wooden blocks, and rolled forward into me and pinned me between the forklift and the column of panels I was preparing!

Honestly, of all the times I have tasted death, none even come close to the feeling that you're about to be crushed to death by a forklift and horse stalls. What an absurd way to die it would have been.

They say in moments like this, your life flashes before your eyes. Not mine. The only thing that flashed before my eyes was the headline "Stupid Rodeo Worker Crushed by Forklift While Working Alone."

In order to avoid such a ludicrous, legendary death, I began to pray to the God of Abraham, Isaac, and Jacob for the strength of Samson to overtake my bones and muscles and cardiovascular system, only instead of helping me destroy an entire army with a donkey's jawbone, I just wanted to be able to push this thing off me and live to run the rodeo arena another day.

Good news. God listened to my little prayer, and the adrenaline kicked in or something so I was able to get my legs tucked up with my feet pressed up against the stall panels and push off the forklift enough for me to drop down and roll out of the way.

WHAT A BRUSH WITH DEATH WILL GIVE YOU

Two things happened that day.

I vowed never to skip leg day again.

I played the best show of my life that night. My band was a sort of screamo-type band, and I definitely screamed louder than I've ever screamed and headbanged my long black hair harder than I've ever headbanged before.

I was alive! On fire! Not literally. But figuratively. Though in hindsight, being on fire would have totally taken that show to the next level.

The movie *Fight Club* has a scene in which Tyler Durden (Brad Pitt) and Jack's Complete Lack of Surprise (Edward Norton) rob a convenience store clerk named Raymond K. Hessel at gunpoint and threaten to kill him if he doesn't start pursuing his dream of becoming a veterinarian. The scene is pretty intense, feels like it's just straight out of nowhere, and is honestly totally psycho, much like the rest of the film. But at the end of the encounter as Raymond runs away, Tyler explains the method to his literal madness, saying, "Tomorrow will be the most beautiful day of Raymond K. Hessel's life. His breakfast will taste better than any meal you and I have ever tasted."[25]

You may have never seen *Fight Club*, and you may have no intention to. That's okay. It's not for everyone, iconic though it may be. But Tyler does have a point—even if the methods of making said point were, let's just say, not quite kosher.

Brushes with death do tend to give us perspective. All of a sudden, all the anxieties and worries we typically have don't seem quite as huge. The molehill-sized mountains get put back in their rightful place. The air just smells a little fresher. The bed is just a little more comfortable. You begin to realize it really is gonna be okay.

The real kicker is when it finally hits you that it was this way all along. Nothing has really changed except your vantage point of life. Our situations and circumstances are always in flux. The one constant is that sometimes life is hard and frustrating and riddled with uncertainties and inconsistencies.

There will always be a better time to pursue your dreams. To leave the job you hate that drains you day in and day out and start doing something you actually love. To finally get married or start a family. Whatever that thing is for you. There will always be excuses. You can always travel more or make more money or do this or that. There will always be obstacles. But something about almost dying kinda makes those excuses and obstacles seem trivial, because they kinda actually are.

LIVE LIKE YOU WERE DYING

So the real question is, how do you make like Tim McGraw and live like you were dying all the time? I mean, I don't have much interest in going 2.7 seconds on a bull named Fu Manchu, but there sure are a lot of things I would do if I were living like I was constantly evading the clutches of death.

During World War II, soldiers on the front lines said that every single meal—even the most mundane ones—tasted exquisite because they knew it might be their last. Every moment had a heightened sense of life about it because they knew it probably wasn't a matter of *if* they were gonna die, but *when* and *how*. The guys who did make it out said that in a really messed-up way, those were the best moments of their lives and it was hard for them to leave that lifestyle. (I told you I was a history fanatic.)

I think the main thing is that when you look at life through that lens, the sense that it's gonna be okay sorta comes into view in living color. It helps us evaluate the things we choose to worry about.

Think about it. If you were gonna die next month or next year or tomorrow . . .

Is winning that argument with your loved one *really* that important?

Does the car you drive really matter that much? (Unless you can drive a classic Land Rover Defender, in which case, yes, it does matter. 'Cause I would definitely wanna drive one of those on my last day.)

Is there someone who needs to know that you love them?

Who do you need to forgive?

Do you really need to work that many hours at the expense of your family or your mental and emotional health?

Do you really want to waste another weekend on the couch?

Are you doing this—whatever this is—because it's true to who you are or because it's what others expect of you?

The list of questions honestly could go on and on. And it probably should.

Would I talk to this person that way if I was gonna die? What if they were gonna die?

Would I harbor bitterness in my heart?

Would I care about the things I think are important now?

Where do I stand with God? How can I be sure?

I don't know about you, but I think I would do things a lot differently if I lived like this. So much so that I think I'm just gonna go ahead and bring this chapter to a close and invite you to take a little inventory yourself.

Maybe get out one of those super-hipster Moleskine notebooks and a craft pen carved from the tusk of a wild boar and just start writing. If all you have is a No. 2 pencil and some printer paper, that'll work too. And if all else fails, there's always the trusty notes app on your phone.

I'll see you in the next chapter.

CHAPTER 11

GETTING AROUND THE SYSTEM

got my first cell phone when I was freshly graduated from high school—a blue Nokia 3310. It was amazing. Having grown up watching Zack Morris of *Saved by the Bell* fame walk around with a brick-sized portable phone, I marveled at the technological miracle I was holding in my hands. Up to that point, all I had personally known was the incessant beeping of the cordless phone waking me up in the middle of the night because my brother had forgotten to hang it up on the battery charger after talking to one of his many "friends who were girls but were not girlfriends." So the fact that I could spend endless hours playing Snake *on my phone* absolutely floored me.

My dad had just bought me a top-of-the-line, steel blue 1976 Buick LeSabre land yacht as a graduation present. It was about 3,500 pounds of pure steel and sex appeal and cost me about a hundred dollars to fill up with gas every two days or so. Nonetheless, it was definitely a luxury to have my own car for the month I got to drive it—until one fateful night as I was driving to Amanda's choir concert, the engine violently began to slam around as copious amounts of smoke billowed from the hood. I pulled over, added a jug of water to the radiator, and turned the key in an effort to make it to my high school sweetheart's show, but Ole Blue was a goner. The engine block had completely melted. I had no way of contacting her to let her know I wasn't gonna make it.

And so the Nokia cell phone became a glorious reality, courtesy of

Verizon and more money than I had ever spent on bills in my life. Four hundred minutes, twenty-five cents per text. Amazing.

Never in my wildest dreams would I have dreamed I could use four hundred minutes on the phone. But I was young, in love, and working by myself at a snow cone stand in Zilker Park. So each morning, I would get on my bicycle and ride the twenty-five miles from the Cedar Valley area just southwest of Austin into downtown, open the stand, make about 150 snow cones, and talk to Amanda. A lot.

Like a whole lot.

This seemed like a great plan. I felt like we were growing closer than ever and were destined to be together! Then one fateful night, I got the bill in the mail: $850.

This was more than I made in a whole month at the snow cone stand. How on earth was I gonna pay for this?

I called to dispute the charges because there was no way on earth I had gone over my limit, only to have them explain that every time the call went to voicemail on her cell phone or the answering machine picked up at her home, it counted as a minute, and I had at least four hundred of those little situations that week alone! I actually cried.

And started looking for a new job.

Amanda was worth it, after all, but I could probably find a job that paid more and at least learn how to let the phone ring three times and hang up before the machine got it and maybe space the calls out from once every twenty minutes to once an hour.

That's how I landed the gas station / pizza shop manager gig. It was a mere two miles from my buddy's house, where I was living, and my boss even let me buy his sweet Honda Accord and make the payments directly to him since I didn't have any credit yet! Plus, the job paid $1,100 a month, which was a big step up for an eighteen-year-old kid!

I moved out of my buddy's house and into a rad fifth-wheel trailer that had no electricity and water that smelled like rotten eggs.

When I woke up with actual icicles on my face, which happened pretty much any time the temperature got below forty degrees, my Nokia would ring and Amanda's dad would invite me to come sleep in their guest room that night to keep warm.

It was kinda crazy getting started out on my own. When you start from scratch, it can tend to be that way. But I worked really hard, didn't take shortcuts, and eventually paid off that cell phone bill. And with each little win, I began to realize that, even with the setbacks, it was gonna be okay.

All along the way, people were there to help. I think there's something to that. As you work hard and try to be a person of integrity and character, you'll often find people who want to jump in and walk alongside you. Guides. Mentors. Coaches. Sages. Teachers. Father figures. They're not gonna beg to teach you, but if you keep yourself humble, teachable, flexible, and honest, you can learn and grow and build a life on their shoulders.

> Sometimes we learn our best lessons making snow cones or pizzas or mucking horse stalls.

Doesn't mean you won't be paying your dues. And probably a whole lot more than you ever thought you would have to. And that's okay because sometimes we learn our best lessons making snow cones or pizzas or mucking horse stalls.

Doesn't mean it won't feel like it's taking forever. And likely a whole lot longer than you ever imagined possible. And that's okay because sometimes the waiting produces the best wine.

But if you stay committed to building your character, you won't be doing it alone.

JIM AND HIS SCALPEL

Jim was one of my guides. In many ways, he was more like a dad to me. I had just started my first job in ministry when Jim found me. He was leading a group of men in our church through memorizing the Bible, and he liked that I seemed to really love the Bible. So he invited me into his circle. We'd meet together each week with his group of guys, and I began to see that this was a dude I wanted to learn from, or more like someone I *needed* to learn from.

I asked him to walk alongside me and teach and mentor me with the hard-earned wisdom he was so full of. He was no-nonsense but tender. He was kind and gentle but not afraid to call me out on my bullcrap anytime he smelled it. And being the young, idealistic, stubborn kid I was, he probably smelled it a lot.

I invited Jim to truly know me. He had full access to tell me what I was doing right and what I could do better. His words cut sometimes, but it was more like a skillful surgeon's scalpel incision than a machete-wielding guerilla warrior hacking away through the underbrush.

We would meet together and I'd tell him my dreams and hopes and vision. He prayed for me, encouraged me, dispensed words of wisdom, and helped me plan out my next steps. He was insanely generous. With his time. With his life. With his words. And with his money.

He was proud of me. He believed in me. And he made sure I knew it.

So much so that if I told him about something I felt God was asking me to do, he would ask what was stopping me. Of course, it almost always boiled down to money. I was a broke musician-pastor with more dreams than funds. But without fail, before that meeting was over, he would ask if he could pay for an album or a sound system or a trailer for my band's gear or a myriad of other things we needed. I never once tried to take advantage of that or position myself to get something from him.

I didn't need to. He was just that kind of generous. God had blessed him, and he wanted to be a blessing to others.

In 2009, I was gearing up for my first full summer of traveling with my band. We had just released our first full-length album and were preparing to leave the last week of May and be gone until the first week of August. While I could bring Amanda and the kids with me for a good bit of it, I would be away from them for a few weeks at a time as well. Jim knew this, and while giving me a hard time about how I was always getting lost because we misread the MapQuest directions we had printed out, he would hint to me that if I would get rid of my little flip phone and get an iPhone, I wouldn't get lost so much and could stay in touch with Amanda and the girls more easily.

I had been casually coveting an iPhone for a while at that point. Growing up, I watched *Star Trek* and was mystified by the idea that people could basically video chat each other from all over the galaxy, and I thought, *How cool would it be if one day I could do that*. Now it was possible with a tiny, handheld device that I could carry around in my pocket! But as much as I was enthralled with the idea of having a phone that would let me talk face-to-face with Amanda and the kids, there was no way I could afford it on my just-starting-out-in-pastoral-ministry salary.

You know when you're planning to get someone you love a freaking amazing Christmas present? You kinda start dropping subtle hints a few months out to whet their appetites, and then when you give it to them, it clicks—that's why you were mentioning it all along. Jim was a master at this. He wasn't busting my chops; he was buttering me up. And when my birthday rolled around that year, he handed me a box and said, "Happy birthday, son. I'm proud of you. I believe in you. And I'm making an investment in you."

Sidenote: there are quite possibly no four words in the English language that are as powerful as "I'm proud of you." If you don't get anything else out of this book, get this: Tell people you're proud of them. They need to hear it.

I opened the box to find a brand-new iPhone staring back at me. I was undone. Speechless. Grace has a way of doing that to people.

And so, equipped with the latest, greatest technology known to creation, I set out with the world literally in the palm of my hand—or the pocket of my jeans, depending on what I was doing at the moment. Until about two weeks in, when I drove onto the blacktop parking lot of a gas station somewhere in the middle of nowhere Kansas. I pulled up alongside the fuel pump and opened the door of our black Chevy Tahoe, and as I was stepping out, my brand-new iPhone fell the three feet from my seat to the blacktop just below, cracking the screen. Nothing crazy. But this was my first iPhone and I couldn't believe it.

Of course, there was no one anywhere around that could fix the phone. It wasn't like it is today. Back then, you had to drive, like, four hundred miles to the closest Apple store. I was gonna have to wait a couple weeks to see the damage. I was sure it was gonna be fine. I had bought the insurance, and this mishap would surely be covered.

Only it wasn't.

When I got home for the weekend and took it to the Apple store, they informed me that broken screens aren't covered by insurance and that it would cost $200 to fix the screen!

Two hundred dollars? Who has two hundred dollars to fix a cracked screen? Not this guy!

I thought, *What a load of* . . . (insert words I won't type here).

I politely asked, "Okay, if broken screens aren't covered, then what is?"

They proceeded to explain that insurance was to cover damages that made the phone unusable.

The gears in my head started turning to interpret these details and figure out a way around the system to get my phone fixed without paying such a ludicrous amount to these money-hungry vipers who probably made the phone screen extra weak just so they could charge countless unsuspecting, clumsy people like me $200 a pop to fix it. Feeling justified in my outrage, I climbed the stairs of a building nearby and threw the phone off the balcony to the ground below, ensuring no one was underneath me and it was safe to do so. Then I walked down the stairs, picked up the broken phone, climbed the stairs again, and threw it overboard once more. This went on for a good ten minutes on repeat—climbing, throwing, retrieving, climbing, throwing, retrieving. You get the point. I got a grocery bag and picked up the pieces of the phone and carried it to the Apple store to find the associate I had spoken with earlier and handed him the bag of iPhone parts with a smirk on my face.

"I think this would qualify as damaged enough to be unusable, right?"

The unsuspecting associate just laughed and looked at me like I was a psycho. Which, to be fair, yeah.

"Sir, this isn't what we meant. Insurance will not cover this! We can't even come close to fixing this. You're gonna have to buy a whole new phone now. It's $800, which is honestly a lot worse than the $200 you would have had to pay an hour ago!"

I stood there livid and more than a little embarrassed. Jim had been so kind and generous in giving me this phone, and now I had squandered it like a hotheaded idiot.

But just as I began to lose hope, a huge sign caught my attention right on the edge of my peripherals.

Open a new line, get an iPhone FREE!

B-I-N-G-O, and Bingo was his name-o. The smirk reappeared.

"So . . . just hear me out."

"Yes?"

"I need to buy a new phone for $800, yeah?"

"Yes?"

"But what if I open a new line? I get the phone free, right?"

"Yes, technically that's true, but . . ."

"Let's open a new line!"

"Okay, but . . ."

"Let's do it."

I signed up for the extra phone line. And got the free phone. For the low, low price of $80 a month on a two-year contract. I paid $1,920 for a line I never used.

When I told Jim, he just shook his head, put his arm around me, and said, "You knucklehead. I love you, son, but you're an idiot. You know better than to trade your character for a little convenience. It never pays off in the end. If you make a mistake, it's gonna be okay. Just own it, man up, and take care of it. Your integrity isn't worth $800, son."

Scalpel.

I needed to hear that. I needed to feel that. The sting of the wound being cleaned and bandaged up.

Jim never brought it up again. Apple never brought it up again. AT&T never brought it up again. In fact, the only person who ever brings it up is me when I'm telling people what an idiot I was, and how I'm still alive and kicking as living proof that failure isn't final. No matter how badly I get it wrong in even the most legendarily idiotic of ways, that's not who I am. I'm not a shattered phone or a $1,920 superfluous phone line. I'm not the same hothead who traded his character for convenience. My failures don't define me; they are refining me. That experience continues to shape me and teach me even to this day.

When you make a mistake, own it and take care of it. It's gonna be okay.

WHO ARE YOU BECOMING?

There is no shortcut or "getting around the system" that's worth your integrity. And let's just be honest. While we've already established that there are no shortcuts, I've yet to find a way to "get around the system" that has actually worked. There's always a cost or a catch, and often it's your character.

It's highly likely that you're not as stupid as I am. I have set a pretty high bar on that particular personality trait. You probably would never destroy a perfectly good, albeit cracked iPhone just to try to get it repaired for free and then open a new line just to avoid paying for a brand-new one, only to pay almost three times the cost. But if I were a betting man, I would guess there are other ways you've been tempted to trade in your character for some convenience.

> Using the corporate card a little loosely, justifying what constitutes a true "business expense" because instead of getting a proper Christmas bonus, you got a crummy greeting card telling you you're the newest member of the Jelly of the Month Club.
> Fudging the numbers on your taxes to stick it to the man and save some money you'd rather put toward a new pool or vacation.
> Copying your book report from Wikipedia or just watching a movie instead and assuming the plot treatment is even close to that of the book.

Lying on your résumé to get a job you really want but are worried you're not qualified for.

Talking about someone behind their back so people will like you more and you'll get the promotion you wanted or you'll be more popular with the in-crowd.

On that note, just a quick rabbit trail word of wisdom. Watch carefully if people talk badly about others around you, because they probably are talking about you like that when you're not around. Gossiping says more about them than the person they're gossiping about.

Trading our character cannibalizes our credibility and creates a lack of trust, which makes it practically impossible to have strong, healthy relationships, let alone truly thrive in the world. For me, the cost was a mere $2,000! In the grand scheme of things, I got off easy when you consider the cost of losing your job, your marriage, your friendships, your freedom as a citizen because you ended up in jail— you know, the usual list that dads give you when they're guilt-tripping you out of doing something super stupid.

I've certainly made much more monumental mistakes since that fateful day with Apple. I've crushed a lot more than a cracked iPhone. I've traded my integrity for fleeting, momentary, idiotic ways of making me feel better about myself, and I have hurt others and broken trust in the process.

And in the end, every single time, without exception, I've learned the hard way how *not worth it* trading away my integrity was.

Maybe you have some experience in that department as well. The pain of the consequences of those decisions doesn't fade easily or quickly. It took me two years to pay off that new iPhone. It's taken me a lot longer to restore trust with the people I have hurt.

Character matters. Not just to you, but to everyone around you. No matter how bright, shiny, and new. No matter how embarrassed you are. No matter how worried and anxious. It's never—not ever—worth trading your character.

There's a Heisenberg in all of us. No matter how much we start out like Walter White. Given the right set and sequence of circumstances, so it is for us.

I know I've probably self-identified as a cinephile ad nauseam at this point and you're probably like, "Okay, okay, we get it, you like movies and stuff." But I feel this distinction gives me a bit of authority when I tell you that *Breaking Bad* is the greatest show of all time. This isn't even an argument. There is no greater example of character development in all of film and television history than Walter White.

I was listening recently to an interview with Bryan Cranston (you know, the sweet, lovable dad from *Malcolm in the Middle*), and he was talking about the creator of *Breaking Bad*, Vince Gilligan, who pitched the show to him and said something to the effect of, "We are gonna turn the good guy into the bad guy." And you watch the show, and it's scary how with every single choice Walter makes, you sort of identify with him like, "Given the circumstances, I probably would have done the same thing."

And little by little, Walter, a lovable chemistry teacher who genuinely cares about his family and wouldn't hurt a fly, becomes Heisenberg, a murderous monster of a drug lord. And it doesn't take long. Just one compromise here and there.

That's me. That's you. There's a Heisenberg in all of us.

Every single seemingly small and insignificant choice of trading in our integrity to help us get by or get around the system turns us, little by little, into someone we weren't before. All of us are always becoming something. The question is, what do you want to become? Rather, *who* do you want to become?

When you come up against a hard decision, always choose the path that keeps your integrity intact. It's gonna be okay. No matter how scary it seems. No matter how hard it is. No matter how costly. Your character costs more. And the person you're becoming deserves that.

CHAPTER 12

IT'S OKAY TO BE WRONG SOMETIMES

know I keep referencing our tenth anniversary trip to London, Paris, and Rome, but it is truly one of my favorite memories of my lifetime. Up to that point, we hadn't really had the opportunity to travel much, and it was just an absolute dream come true.

But of all the stories we tell from that trip, the one about the compote is still the one that makes the rounds most frequently.

I had never had a proper English breakfast. In fact, I hadn't had much of a proper anything at all. Growing up, when we wanted to celebrate at a fancy restaurant, our golden ticket was Golden Corral. All you can eat steak for, like, eight dollars! You can't beat that!

So when we woke up to our first morning in London, we were more than a little excited to try a proper English breakfast.

The waiter brought out our plates, each boasting two fried eggs, baked beans, a couple of sausages, a slice of back bacon, blood pudding, tomatoes (or tomahtoes as they would say), mushrooms, and some fried breads. We were quite surprised because everything we had read said that Americans' portions were ginormous compared to the rest of the world, but this was by far the largest breakfast either of us had ever seen.

And then there was the compote.

To me this little condiment looked like a jam. Or possibly like a really upscale pie filling you might put on top of a stack of superfroofy pancakes at the International House of Pancakes. But it was definitely labeled compote.

"Hmmm. I bet this compoatee is really good on this bread."

It was like a record scratch, and Amanda stopped midbite, looked up from her food, and just started laughing. Not with me. At me.

"Compoatee?"

"Yeah, compoatee! It says it right here!"

"It's compote. Like com-POAT. You don't say the *e* on the end."

I had no clue how to say this word, but I was fairly certain I had heard it pronounced *my* way before. Maybe it was the Philip Seymour Hoffman movie *Capote* that was getting me all confused. But I couldn't accept defeat.

"Yeah, I don't think that's how you say it. I think it's got a hard *e* on the end. It's more European that way," I said, continuing to plead my case.

"It's not more European. It's just more *not correct*," she quipped back with a playful, flirty smirk on her face.

I whipped out my trusty phone, connected to the hotel Wi-Fi, and commenced googling how to pronounce compote to see who was right. This is kinda how things go in our house. We are both very strong-willed, opinionated, and completely opposite persons in every way except the ones that matter most. So even things like how to say a word like *compote* can turn into an Olympic sport.

It's amazing how sometimes with words, you can google how to say it and find a few different takes on it.

Like *yolk*, for example. Some takes have the *l* silent, while in others the *l* is more pronounced.

Some people pronounce *coupon* as "kewpon / q-pon" instead of "coopon."

There are a ton of words with varied pronunciations like this: *melk, pellow, bolth, expecially, expresso*. Words that often have a hard *t* versus instances where the *t* is silent. You know, the usual suspects.

But you know what *no one on earth* says? *Compoatee*. Not a one. It's *compote*. No *e* on the end.

Like if you looked up the word in a dictionary, there would probably be a picture of me with a caption: "This idiot is literally the only person in the world who ever thought this word wasn't just straight up *compote*."

Amanda owned me on this one. Like it wasn't even close. But as if the defeat weren't already a total fatality, I heard the voice of the announcer from *Mortal Kombat* shout, "Finish him!" just before she lowered the final blow.

"Don't worry, Stephen, at least you know that Adam and Eve had skin now."

This phrase means absolutely nothing to you yet. But it will. Just give me a second to explain.

ADAM AND EVE

I grew up in the church and honestly loved Jesus for just about as far back as I can remember. My mom saw to it that I was there every Sunday morning, Sunday night, Wednesday night supper followed by youth group, Thursday morning men's prayer breakfast, and Friday night lock-in, not to mention puppet ministry, youth choir, Royal Ambassadors, mission trips, and Vacation Bible School. If the doors were open, I was there.

I definitely went through phases when I just wanted to fake being sick so I could stay home and play *Duck Hunt* on our new Nintendo, or eventually, once we were able to borrow a friend's Nintendo 64, *GoldenEye*—the greatest game of all time.

But the 99.9 percent of the other times when I wasn't playing hooky, I was in church, and other than the terrible music, I actually liked learning about Jesus. So I would read my Bible at home, and one day when I was maybe eleven, a particular line stood out to me, which I underlined in my oh so cool Teen Study Bible with the F.R.O.G. (Fully Rely on God) Bible cover.

It was the account of the fall in Genesis when Adam and Eve had just sinned against God and God basically said, "You had one job!"

He graciously covers their nakedness and promises to protect them, in spite of the devastating consequences of their actions, and essentially for the first time in history, "It's gonna be okay" is spoken to encourage the ones he loves. He tells them that the stinking idiot serpent that deceived them was gonna have its head crushed by a freaking amazing Savior who would come one day to set humanity free from all the sin and sickness and death and darkness that was coming into the world.

It's actually a gorgeous passage that gives me more hope than just about any other passage in the whole Bible. Because it's the picture of a loving Father holding his kids who have just messed up royally and telling them he still loves them and it's gonna be okay. That speaks to me. Because I'm the idiot kid who eats the only dadgum fruit I wasn't supposed to eat out of an *entire garden* of the most luscious fruit imaginable.

And yet in my eleven-year-old mind, I didn't catch *any of that*! You know what *my* takeaway was?

When I read Genesis 3:21—"The LORD God made garments of skin for Adam and his wife and clothed them"—my little preteen brain interpreted this to mean that before they messed up, they didn't have skin. How this works, well, I never even took another step in that thought process to work it out. But my mind was so utterly blown.

This little tidbit of theological *gold* lodged itself in my mind and somehow just never shook loose.

So when seven years later, I had Amanda out on a hot date that consisted of a movie followed by some buffalo wings and fried pickles accompanied by my favorite of all foods—ranch dressing—there came a moment when the conversation kinda hit a lull and I started reaching for ways to impress her.

"You know, Amanda, before the fall, Adam and Eve didn't have skin."

If only I could have had a Zack Morris "time-out."

1. What a dork!
2. I wish I had a time machine to go back and tell myself to rethink my assumptions and not say the thing I was about to say.
3. This is not the best way to impress a girl. No matter how much of a church kid you are.

She proceeded to react in a way I have seen entirely too many times since. Slowly pulling away from her lips the bite she was about to take, she cocked her head to the side and squinted slightly as a grin spread across her lips, which hesitantly uttered, "What?"

Me, knowing in my heart of hearts that I had just gotten her attention and was about to impress her, well, I doubled down, repeating my revelation.

"Before the fall, Adam and Eve didn't have skin!" I said with a bit of a know-it-all, are-you-impressed-yet grin on my face.

As diplomatically as she knew how, she said, "What are you talking about?"

"Well, Genesis 3 says that after they ate the fruit, they realized they were naked and God clothed them with skin! So I don't know if it was just like something with the atmosphere or something that changed after the fall or what, but apparently they didn't need skin before and now they did, so God gave them skin!"

I could hardly contain my giddiness. This girl was gonna marry me. Or at least kiss me. Okay, maybe just a nice little Christian side hug.

"So, what?" she baited me. "They were just like bones and organs walking around?"

"Yeah, I guess so. I mean, I guess God just kinda held it all together somehow!"

She couldn't contain herself.

"He clothed them with skins, with an *s*. Like animal skins! He made them clothes!"

Suddenly, it occurred to me that I had never even thought about that passage in seven years and my eleven-year-old outlook on life was still permeating my mind, unchallenged and unchanged until this very moment. This preteen assumption had somehow made its way into my eighteen-year-old brain, and Amanda had just completely shattered it with one single sentence. It's amazing how quickly the light bulb went off, and I was instantly more embarrassed than I have ever been in my life—which is saying something for a guy who doesn't get embarrassed.

"Ooooohhhhhh! That makes total sense! Man, I hadn't even thought about that. I read it when I was like eleven and have just sorta lived with that assumption ever since."

We had a good laugh about it and just about once a month, every month, for the last twenty years, we have laughed about it. Well, *she* has laughed about it. Usually, it's the trump card to remind me that just because I assume I'm right about something doesn't mean I am, and I really do need to think critically about it. Like when I googled the pronunciation of *compote*. It's one of those cautionary tales of my stupidity that keeps me humble and helps me to never be too sure of my own opinion on anything.

It's okay to be wrong. It's okay to not know. It's gonna be okay if you have to rethink your position on a variety of subjects throughout your entire life.

It's also okay to not let getting it wrong become your identity. Like I'm not walking around all the time feeling beat down because I thought Adam and Eve didn't have skin or that compote was pronounced a certain way. That wasn't final. That wasn't who I am. It didn't define me, but it has refined me and helped me realize that being wrong is inherently part of being human. I don't have to be right. And what I may have been right about a few years ago, I may not be right about now. The great lyricist Bob Dylan sums it up oh so well: "The times they are a-changin'."[26]

Sometimes you change. Sometimes the world changes around you.

IF YOU STAND FOR NOTHING, YOU'LL FALL ON A TOADSTOOL

I once made a reference to Princess Toadstool from *Super Mario Bros.* I had grown up playing this game and I knew that I knew that I knew that this was her name. But my kids just looked at me like I was crazy.

"Dad, who the heck is Princess Toadstool?"

"The princess in *Mario*!"

"Don't you mean Princess Peach?"

"I mean, I'm pretty sure her name is Princess Toadstool."

"That's a terrible name, Dad. That's definitely not her name. She's Princess Peach."

But this was a hill I was willing to die on. Because, you know, you gotta have principles. If you stand for nothing, you'll fall for anything.

"Kids, I grew up playing that game. It's freaking Princess Toadstool. Hey, Siri, what's the name of the princess in *Mario*?"

Siri is my personal assistant. She's Australian, and in most cases she can tell me the answer to my questions and settle things outright, right then and there.

"The name of the princess in *Super Mario Bros.* is Princess Peach."

Hmmmm. This can't be right. So I did a little digging. And it turns out we were both right! Her full name is Princess Peach Toadstool. If you'll allow me to geek out for a second, I find this little excerpt from Wikipedia far too interesting:

> In Japan, Peach's name has always been Princess Peach (ピーチ姫, *Pīchi-Hime*, Princess Peach) since her debut in the original *Super Mario Bros.* in 1985, but she was localized as "Princess Toadstool" in the English-language manual. The English version of *Yoshi's Safari*, released in 1993, contained the first usage of the name "Peach" in the Western world, though she was called Princess Toadstool in *Wario Land: Super Mario Land 3*, released in 1994. In *Super Mario 64*, released in 1996, she uses both names in a letter addressed to Mario, signing it "Peach." From the 1996 game *Mario Kart 64* onward, the name Peach is used in Western versions.[27]

Thanks to that little conversation, I learned something new that day. And so did my kids. And not just that "wow, Dad is really old."

I honestly think this kind of open-minded, curious conversation, with a willingness to strive for humble grace, whether you're wrong or right, is one of the great keys to life. I might have felt like I was taking crazy pills if I turned out to be completely wrong and was just imagining a weirdo name like Toadstool, but at least I would know.

CLING TO THE TRUTH

As much as I probably act like a know-it-all sometimes, if there's one thing I'm learning as I get older, it's that I don't actually *know much* at all. I think a lot of things. I assume a lot. I have opinions and preferences. But I'm trying to stay curious, open, honest with myself, and willing to change my mind about important things and some not-so-important ones.

To do that, I'm finding I have to cling to the truth and let the truth cling to me.

A few years back, my band was playing at a conference in a stadium in Louisiana, and when we got there, the guy at the front door put a stamp on my hand that gave me access to get backstage. But before you play, no one knows who you are. You know who you are, but everyone else couldn't care less.

A few times, I was asked by some fairly scary-looking stadium security workers in not the nicest tone to show my hand to prove I was allowed to be where I was. For all they knew, I could have been some psycho stalker, fiendishly preying on my celebrity obsession. They were just doing their job to keep me from being a news headline or worse the next day. So I lifted my arm to show off the black circle stamped on the back of my hand. And I got to carry my stuff in, snag a Pamplemousse LaCroix and some beef jerky (my preferred snack before singing, because carbs hate me), and relax on the greenroom couch.

That stamp was my access. Not because it was convenient or cool.

Not because it was an altogether IG-worthy, rad design. No one was gonna look at it and ask me how many hours I was in the chair at some super-trendy tattoo shop and what it meant. No, it was my access because of the truth it represented. So I clung to that stamp that week to prove the truth of my identity.

But as much as I clung to it, that stamp clung to me. Like, annoyingly so. I took a shower after the first night, and it was still there. I took a shower on the second morning after my workout, and it wouldn't come off. Morning after morning, night after night, it stayed with me and we were like Forrest and Jenny as kids—peas and carrots. That stamp clung to the skin on my hand for a whole dadgum week! But you know what? It became a symbol to me of so much more than backstage access. It reminded me of the truth that I belonged.

When I say "the truth," I'm not using some ethereal, loosey-goosey term to sound more philosophical. I very intentionally mean those unchanging realities that act as our compass and our true north.

As a Christian, I would be inauthentic if I didn't at least mention that I see the truth through the foundational lens of the Bible, which I believe to be God's Word—his love letter to me through which I can truly know him and know how he created me and the world around me to run and know where I stand with him for all of eternity. In the Bible, I see that Jesus himself is the truth. That he is God, that he loves me, that he died on the cross so I could live forever in heaven, and that he takes care of me, giving and guiding, protecting and providing. This is as real as gravity or the wind. Invisible. Mysterious. Yet ever-present and evident.[28]

And if you'd allow me, I want to quickly encourage you to see for yourself. If you don't have a copy of the Bible, shoot me a note on Instagram. I'll get your address and send you a copy. That's how much I believe it'll change your life.

Beyond that, you don't have to necessarily be a Jesus follower like me to know that truth is real and evident. Like gravity, the truth really isn't as abstract of a phrase as we like to make it. Sure, we may have different perspectives or opinions on the truth. We may or may not like it, and we may or may not want to believe it. But the truth doesn't change based on that perspective. In staying the same, truth centers us with its reliability and gives us boundaries within which we can flourish with boundless liberty.

The truth, after all, sets us free, whereas the lack thereof just leads to confusion and chaos. Like if you're trying to find your way out of a place with one exit (and everyone has a different opinion on where it is), you may have a hard time finding your way out if you listen to every "I think it's that way" that enters your ears. There is a difference between truth and assumptions. And there is a difference between unwavering facts and fickle feelings.

> Sometimes truth will feel like a warm hug, and sometimes it'll feel like a kick in the teeth.

Sometimes the truth will feel like a limitation, but in reality, it's an opportunity. Like a speed limit, for example. That's a clear, objective truth—a law even. When the authorities over us have clearly marked what is right and wrong and we step outside of it, there are consequences. That can feel like a frustrating burden, especially when we're running late or are impatient by nature. But that 70 miles per hour speed limit is there to protect us and everyone around us as we drive this magnificent miracle of a modern invention called the automobile. Sometimes the truth limits us for our good.

Sometimes truth will feel like a warm hug, and sometimes it'll feel like a kick in the teeth. When I was in high school, my youth pastor at church came up to me with a Bible and hit me over the head and said, "Truth hurts, don't it?" It was a really bad dad joke, but it was a funny illustration of a popular saying that has stuck with me all these years later. *Truth hurts, don't it.*

I know I keep coming back to *Ted Lasso* quotes, but I was watching an episode on the treadmill recently to make the monotony of being on a rat wheel go faster and thought this one particular scene was so fitting as I prepared to write this chapter. Dr. Sharon Fieldstone, the team therapist, tries to get this point across to Ted in a therapy session: "The truth will set you free, but first it will piss you off."[29] I paused my run for a second so I could grab my phone and write it down in my notes app. And no, not *just* because I was looking for an excuse to stop running for a few minutes.

The truth isn't always what we *want* to hear. But it is always what we *need* to hear.

Sometimes the truth will be nuanced and require some critical thinking to flesh out what it looks like in real life. Not everything is as black-and-white as we want it to be, and people's experiences are so different.

Sometimes truth will challenge the long-held assumptions you've had lodged up in that brain of yours for decades, and sometimes it'll paint your skies and oceans and mountains with colors you didn't even know existed.

But in the end, it is the truth—not my feelings, assumptions, opinions, or cultural relevance—that is an anchor when the storms of life come. When depression or anxiety or fear invades and you don't know what to do. When success comes flooding into your life and you have more blessing than you know how to wisely handle. When your circumstances change, the truth doesn't, and so it's uniquely qualified to be there as your steady anchor when you need it most. My feelings change based on what I ate or didn't eat that day, and you know what they say about assumptions.

Opinions and cultural relevance are only consequential for the season in which they are held. The goatee I wore from 2001 to 2011 is not cool anymore. Neither are the wide-leg parachute pants I wore in high school or the Jonathan Taylor Thomas–inspired chili bowl haircut I gave myself in sixth grade to try to fit in. And Golden Corral, despite making gluttony affordable, no longer constitutes the height of luxury for me.

Cultural norms existed a hundred years ago that you'd be destroyed for today. And in a hundred years, the things we call normal today will be considered barbaric figments of a caveman's imagination. Culture changes. Feelings change. Truth doesn't. So we don't bend the truth to align with our emotions or our culture. We align our culture and our feelings to stay in step with the truth.

It's okay if in our pursuit of the truth we find ourselves a little too embarrassed about some of the things we *thought* were true. I promise you, the absurdity of thinking Adam and Eve didn't have skin is no small embarrassment. But it's a regular reminder that I can never be too sure of myself to the extent that I stop pursuing the truth. And when I find it, or rather when it finds me (the truth is not playing hard to get but is actually looking for us!), I don't have to be afraid to adjust to it. It doesn't make me weak. It doesn't make me stupid. On the contrary, to blow up and say, "No, I'm right," and view with contempt the invitation to align myself with what's true—that would be stupid.

But the truth isn't a hammer to beat people with, nor is it a shovel to bury them with. As satisfying as it can be to be right, it's far better to be kind. Everyone is on this journey of life together—finding meaning and purpose—and we're all trying to figure it out. All our baggage and brokenness, blind spots and biases, weaknesses and wounds.

Our experiences are all so different, and yet one thing is true for each of us: our experiences shape the way we see the world, ourselves, God, each other, you name it.

If you're reading this and feeling like I'm stepping on your toes or getting on my soapbox, this isn't my intention. I'm not trying to preach at anyone or force anything down anyone's throat. I find myself burdened to write this because too many times in my life I have known what is right and true and chosen to believe something different, and the consequences have been quite painful—not just for me but for people around me as well.

Similarly, others in our lives—from close friends to people we don't even know personally—have done the same, and it has impacted our family, sometimes in devastating ways. So I suppose this chapter feels a little more serious, because it actually is.

LOVING CONVERSATIONS IN THE PURSUIT OF TRUTH

The world feels more divided than ever, and it feels more crucial than ever that we find a way to look into our own souls and become aware of the truth that we are all processing together. No one was ever bludgeoned into believing like you do. All the shaming and screaming on Facebook pages and Twitter profiles doesn't really lead to real change. But having loving conversations over coffee or dinner or a great bourbon or a proper English breakfast where we decide together to pursue the truth, even if we're coming at it from drastically different perspectives, may just be the key.

Every day is an opportunity to challenge our assumptions, dethrone our preferences as the ultimate say, recognize that culture isn't always the wisest arbiter of truth, and just decide that no matter what, we are all in this thing together.

I know at this point I probably sound like a tree-hugging hippie or something. But what I'm getting at is that as idealistic as I am, I think

I'm just too old to be idealistic about myself. I have made way too many mistakes and thought about things all wrong far too many times. My pursuit of truth has led me to conclusions I've had to reassess or discard with time. The stuff I was so sure about in my teens and twenties just feels a lot less black-and-white and a lot more ROYGBIV. I used to know everything. Now I realize I know nothing. Maybe you know the feeling.

It's the not knowing that makes life an adventure. The not knowing—the seeking of truth, the pursuit of truth—brings a humility that allows us to truly enjoy the discovery. And that's the common journey all of us are on. So let's walk it together with kindness and let the truth find us.

CHAPTER 13

TRYING *WAY* TOO HARD!

o be honest, Stephen, you just kinda blend in with all the other young bands out there. There's nothing really setting you apart. You sound just like them. Look just like them. You have to do something to stand out."

I sat there in all my twenty-four-year-old angst across from a music consultant I had hired to help me take my band to the next level, nodding and trying to take it all in without being offended. This is the kind of thing industry professionals tell you must be done in order to make it in the music business. Even as a Christian artist, apparently having a good heart and motives while being pretty good at what you do doesn't matter all that much. You have to have the look.

I had been grinding it out in overtime. For a couple years when I was first getting started as a musician, the band and I were playing five nights a week, and at this point we were doing every weekend plus whole months at a time in the summer. It was intense. This was years before Spotify. YouTube was just getting going as a social media platform, and our channel wouldn't even exist for at least another 144 months. The tools we so easily and conveniently use to discover bands nowadays weren't a thing back then. And though I was able to say something a lot of musicians don't get to—that I'm a full-time musician and that I provide for my family in this way—it just wasn't quite enough for me. I was like Ariel from *The Little Mermaid*. I wanted moooooooooore.

The consultant opened a lookbook of sorts and started walking me through things we could do to stand out. This was before Pinterest took off, so he had printed out photos of shirts, shoes, pants, glasses, jackets, and more, organizing them neatly in a three-ring binder with his analysis of ways we could improve our chances of making it big.

"Here are the shoes you wanna get. Shoes matter. These sneakers will help you go to the next level. Everyone is doing Chuck Taylors these days. You really want these Nikes. Pair that with a nice suit, and you're in business. Also, you need to shed some pounds. Your music is good, but there's not room for another fat guy in Christian music."

I called a meeting with the band guys to discuss our new wardrobe.

"So basically we are the Jonas Brothers," I said. "No more T-shirts. No more jeans. We suit up every time. You can still wear Chucks, but you gotta have a tie and a jacket or vest on. We shop at Express now, boys."

And for the next few months, Express got way too much of our money.

If I sound like I was insecure and fame hungry, it's because I kinda was. My motives were alloyed—mostly good, but I had a massive hole in my soul from my past wounds. I felt like I needed to prove myself by becoming a super-mega-successful Christian worship musician. I knew the right things to say, but I did stupid stuff, like dress like the JoBros to try to make it. I wanted to show everyone that I was worthy of getting into the most-successful-Christian-artists-of-all-time club.

I was trying way too hard.

It was absolutely bonkers. I don't think back on those days with any kind of pride whatsoever, and I actually wrote a whole book about my struggle to break loose from being the world's biggest approval vampire: *Worship Leaders, We Are Not Rock Stars.*[30]

Sidenote: if you're unfamiliar with what a worship leader is, put simply, it's the person who leads people in singing music about and to God at church and Christian faith-based events. Alternative titles for this particular role could be song leader, psalmist, lead worshiper, music leader, music minister, worship pastor, worship minister, music pastor—and the list goes on. But that should put things in perspective about how pathetic the notion of being a "famous" worship leader is. For that to be one's aim is sorta missing the point.

Nonetheless, the meeting with this consultant came just in time to adjust our plans for the summer and walk into a full eleven weeks of playing youth camps all over the South dressed to the nines. Sure, it was 110 degrees outside, and a few of the venues didn't even have air conditioning in their main gathering rooms. Sure, we were hanging out with a bunch of kids for the week who were all wearing only workout clothes and swimsuits. But we were dedicated to sweating our patooties off day in and day out if there was even a chance that anyone would see us.

We finished our summer commitment, and Roger, the director of one of those camps, called for a little chat.

"Hey, Stephen, how does it feel to try way too hard to impress a bunch of kids with a three-piece suit all summer in the 100-degree heat?"

Roger didn't mince words and pulled no punches. He was a mountain of a man with blazing red hair and the kind of deep voice that travels through the phone right into your very soul. He was assertive and direct, but kind. And you knew he cared about you when he talked to you. He was the head of a camp organization that had hired the band for several weeks that summer. And this wasn't just any camp. It was *the* camp. Like, the one everyone wants to do. He could have hired anyone, but he hired me and the guys. And I was making a fool of myself.

"Well, you know, man . . . I uh . . . I just . . . uhhh . . . We just wanted to try something new, you know?" I gave him a few other super-weak excuses, and he just listened.

"Stephen, you know I care about you. I want to see you succeed. You're just getting started, and I want to help. You know what's gonna make you stand out? It's not dressing like the Jonas Brothers. It's caring about people, being really good at what you do, and showing them Jesus. You've got those down. Stick to that. And don't ever wear a suit at camp again, bro."

And I never did.

But about a year later, the hole in my soul and, consequently, the hunger to go to the next level was still driving me as strongly as ever. I wasn't wearing super-trendy *GQ* model suits with tennis shoes anymore, but I still had my eyes on "making it" as a "famous worship leader." I had already begun employing my old tactics to get booked to play at clubs and venues when I was doing those kinds of gigs. But now I was researching big churches and Christian conferences and events I could send my music to so I'd get to lead worship there. *The bigger the church or event, the more people I get my music in front of, the bigger impact I can make for the glory of God*, I would tell myself.

And there was one white whale I was eyeing. I had heard about a college Bible study in my home state of Texas that had about ten thousand college students attending every week. I just knew that if I could get a crack at playing for this Bible study, it would be the silver bullet that would catapult my career as a famous rock star worship leader.

I went about my usual routine of finding the point of contact and sending my CD with an exquisitely designed, full-color, four-panel press kit, complete with professional photos of the band, top-shelf biography, curated testimonials, and contact information.

In this particular case, Ben was the guy to talk to. I called every single week, asking for him.

"Hey, yes, this is Stephen Miller. I sent you my album and a little package of info about my band and myself, and I'd love to talk to Ben about the possibility of leading worship for your event."

His assistant listened quietly week after week, and each week, she responded, "I'm sorry, he's not in right now. I can deliver the message, and he'll call you back."

Time passed, and a call never came. So by that time the next week, I figured it was worth it to call back. No one ever got anything without persistence, right?

"Hi, it's Stephen Miller again. Just calling to make sure Ben received the album I sent him. I'd love to talk if he has a few moments to connect."

Same response.

He never called back.

This probably went on for a good three months until it kinda became a point for me to prove. It felt like a direct assault on my worth, and so I just decided to double down. When you tell someone you're gonna call them back, you should actually do it. You can't just dismiss people and brush them off. If you don't want to talk to me, just tell me.

I'm guessing they decided the same thing and felt they needed to finally speak up to the kid who just wouldn't take the hint.

"Hi! It's Stephen Miller. Can I speak to Ben?"

"Look, man," his assistant finally leveled with me, "you're trying way too hard. If he wants to call you, he'll call you. But you can't just keep calling and annoying people to try to get a gig. We get a dozen calls like this every week. If we want you to lead worship for us, you'll know it. But until that day comes—if it does—please stop calling. Until then, maybe chill out and be content where you are."

Initially, the sting of rejection was searing. Somehow, subconsciously, all the times I had been told I wasn't good enough came rushing in. And yet, simultaneously, the pain washing over me opened my eyes to that same conversation from a year earlier. I *was* trying way too hard. I had been my entire life.

I couldn't sleep that night. I tossed and turned until I couldn't take it anymore. I got up and paced the living room for hours, having it out with God and trying to figure out what in the world I was supposed to do with my life!

I believe God truly cares about me and my life, even the small things, like when I'm brokenhearted and hurting. And so that night, it felt as though God was meeting me in my living room to comfort me and give me peace. Not peace to justify my continuing to try way too hard. Not peace to keep trying to prove I mattered and had worth. But peace to understand the truth that I already had worth and value apart from my accomplishments and that as long as I was looking to prove I mattered, I was just gonna keep being robbed of the joy of knowing I mattered anyway. Peace to know it was gonna be okay.

WHAT HAS COMPARISON BROUGHT YOU?

I didn't need to waste any more time comparing myself with other successful Christian musicians or worship leaders. I didn't need to wonder when it was gonna be my turn to make it. I didn't need to be the one playing at that next big conference or event or having my song on the radio or climbing the charts. I didn't need crowds of fans or followers or attaboys or applause. I was already fully loved, adored, and cherished by God, who had already decisively proven it by dying for me on a cross and rising from the dead.

But even if I didn't come from a place of faith where I believe that is true of me, what good would it do me to play a comparison game that only robbed me of my joy? What good does the comparison game ever do?

How does looking at someone else's success and wishing I had it ever make me happier?

How does seeing someone else on vacation and asking, "Why can't that be me?" add any joy to my life?

Has being envious of someone's home or car or career or vacation or relationship ever brought me *more* peace? Or just less? I don't know about you, but envy like that has never brought me more peace. Not once.

It's been said that comparison is the thief of joy. It's like a disease that just takes and takes and takes, stealing our energy and strength.

But contentment is the antidote to comparison. And contentment goes hand in hand with gratitude.

Yet, and possibly because of this, contentment seems harder and harder to come by. Especially in this day of social media where people only show the highlights, it's easier than ever to feel like what you have isn't quite enough. Your house isn't Pinteresty enough. Your kids aren't polite enough. Your marriage or relationship isn't romantic enough. You're not fit enough or pretty enough or hot enough. You're not talented enough or wealthy enough.

> Contentment is the antidote to comparison.

I still struggle with this myself. Not in the same way I used to, but it's still there. I wish I could say I've learned the secret of contentment, but to be honest, I've spent most of my life wishing for more. Some call it wanderlust. I don't know if I would consider it worthy of a word so whimsical.

But in my quest to remind myself and everyone else that it's gonna be okay, I wrote a song, and it's kinda become the closing anthem of every video for the last two years on our YouTube channel. It's called "Home."

There's a million miles I've traveled in my head,
I can't shake the need for somewhere else instead.

God, be my refuge, come calm my heart.
You are my home.

There's a million things I wish were different,
Because even from this hell I'm heaven-bent.
God, be my refuge, come calm my heart.
You are my home

For your name's sake,
you will lead me back home to you.

There's a longing in me I can't satisfy.
I got nothing here to show for all my strife.
God, be my refuge, come calm my heart.
You are my home.

For your name's sake,
you will lead me back home to you.

My greener pastures, my quiet waters,
Here at your table, I couldn't want more.
When mountains crumble and oceans roar,
Here at your table, I couldn't want more.

For your name's sake,
you will lead me back home to you.

The truth is, in most cases, we truly have all we need already. The grass is already greener where we are. The waters are already quiet where we are. We simply need to reorient our perspective. Gratitude helps us do that. It leads us to a place of contentment. It leads us to a place of joy. It leads us to a place of peace where we don't feel the need to try too hard to prove anything.

When I was in high school, I used to watch a kids' TV show because my little cousins watched it, and, consequently, the second I had children of my own, you can bet your bottom dollar I was watching it with them! It was called *VeggieTales on TV*, and it was definitely better than the alternatives of *Barney*, *The Wiggles* (though I still sing that catchy "Fruit Salad" song), or—the craziest one of all—*Teletubbies*.

The episode of *VeggieTales* called "Madame Blueberry" had a particularly catchy song I still sing to this day (the "Thankfulness Song") that includes the line, "A thankful heart is a happy heart."[31]

Thinking back, if I had just been singing this to myself all along, perhaps I could have saved myself the heartache of being told on what seems like more than a hundred occasions, "Bro, you're trying too hard."

If I had just reminded myself to be grateful for who I was, how I was, where I was, when I was, and what I had, perhaps I could have saved myself a lot of sleepless nights with my head in my hands, crying, "Why not me?"

This isn't to say you shouldn't dream or work or have vision or drive. I do believe you should be the hardest worker in the room and that you should always stay hungry. But I also think we miss out on a lot of the wonder, awe, amazement, satisfaction, and delight of the things we are and have because we can't keep our eyes off the things we aren't and don't have.

The good news is, this is a daily choice. Possibly even a minute-by-minute, second-by-second choice. No matter how badly I get it wrong, my failure isn't final. I'll have another shot at it as soon as the second hand on my watch clicks into place again here in a sec.

My lack of contentment and gratitude is not who I am. Even if I'm a historically ungrateful person, I can choose this very moment to believe I am enough and I have enough and to be thankful for every last morsel of life and molecule of oxygen that has been given to me because I sure as heck can't make oxygen on my own.

My struggle with contentment doesn't define me, but it can refine me. It's the very struggle that pushes us and causes us to grow. If we let it, it can reveal to us all the things we've been hoping will satisfy us that could never satisfy. If we let it, it can pull back the curtain on the things we have been trusting in that will only disappoint us. If we don't give up and don't give in, it can lead beyond the frustrating futility of trying way too hard or pining for bigger and better things to true, lasting joy and contentment.

PIVOTAL MOMENT

Fast-forward fifteen years since those weekly calls with Ben's assistant and Ben and I are friends now. We did a youth camp together recently, and in a Q and A we did together, I told the story to a bunch of kids about how I used to call him over and over and over and over, trying to get him to book me to lead worship for his Bible study, only to get the brush-off.

We just laughed, and while Ben apologized, I thanked him and told the audience that as much as it hurt, it was one of the most important, pivotal moments of my life. It helped me, in concert with a myriad of other experiences, to see that I could stop trying way too hard to prove I was worth something, because I was, in fact, actually worth something already.

And so are you.

You have worth and value far beyond anything you can comprehend.

You have been created by a God who loves you—and doesn't just love you; he *likes* you!

Let me say that a bit louder for the people in the back. *God doesn't just love you; he likes you!*

He's not begrudgingly tolerating you because he has to. He's God! No one can force him to do anything. He's not just waiting for you to screw up again so he can crush you. He lovingly created you because it made him happy to do so. He looks at you like a really good Father who is just so proud of his kid—grinning from ear to ear with joy welling up in his heart every time he sees you. You can't earn or create a better identity than that!

God gave you unique gifts and personality and passions because he wanted to. He sent Jesus to die on a cross to pay for your sins so that you could be completely forgiven of everything you have ever and ever will do wrong—every single mess-up, mix-up, epic fail, or whatever—and live with him forever in a place where there is no sin or sickness, death or darkness. A place with no backstabbing friends or corrupt politicians. A place with no rush-hour traffic when your AC doesn't work and it's 110 degrees outside or being put on hold for what feels like hours only to be transferred to someone who has no idea what they're talking about or accidently hangs up on you so you have to start all over. A place where you never have to fold kids' laundry or peel boiled eggs again. (Can I get a hallelujah?) There is only beauty and perfection, and we are completely healed, whole, and happy—*forever*. Because God himself will be with us in ways we could never comprehend, and he doesn't allow all that crap to invade his presence. But he sure does love you, like you, and want you to be there.

Stop trying too hard and letting all that other stuff define you. Let it push you to realize who you were really created to be. That's the greener pastures and the quiet waters. That's where the real life is at.

A LITTLE MORE GRACE

debated on writing this sort of mini chapter, but since I'm a dad, I guess I just feel compelled to share a few final thoughts.

As I've written this book the last few months, I've honestly been blown away that I'm still alive. In fact, I've read these chapters along the way to my wife, my kids, a couple friends, and even my publisher, and at some point each of them has said, "Wow, I can't believe you're still alive." I concur.

Some variations have been uttered, such as, "Wow, I can't believe you were so dumb." This one hurt a bit more, but I have to agree with the sentiment.

And I'm sure some even thought, *Wow, how were you allowed to procreate?* Which, to be fair—true . . .

To these questions, I can give no real answer except that my statement on which this entire book is written is simply true: *it's gonna be okay.*

I'm still alive because it's gonna be okay.

I'm probably the dumbest person most people have ever met, and yet it's gonna be okay.

I procreated, and yet it's gonna be okay—as evidenced by the amazing offspring that came as the result.

I'm truly grateful the internet wasn't really in full swing when the majority of these stories originated. I am even more grateful that my life has, for the most part, been spent in obscurity, outside of the limelight of even such an odd platform as YouTube.

For all our grasping and grabbing and grappling, the world tends to write our victories in the sand while etching our failures in concrete. And as I ponder this, I am truly thankful that I've been afforded the ability to be a normal human being who makes not-so-normal stupid decisions without the entire world knowing every detail of every second of my failures.

But the same thing is true about me now as it was then. I am flawed, broken. Sometimes devastatingly so. And so are you, though I assure you I am worse yet. I mean, did you read this book? And that's just the tip of the iceberg.

But maybe, just maybe, you see a bit of yourself in these stories. Maybe you can identify with the foot-in-your-mouth feeling after saying something offensive or even downright damnable.

Maybe you see yourself in the idiotic antics or moments of wildly jockeying for worth.

My hope was that this book would be a bit of a mirror—but one of those circus mirrors that shows you the weirdest versions of yourself. One that sorta puts the real you into focus by showing you the most absurd version in contrast.

That's me. I'm the weirdest possible goober version of you. And yet, for whatever reason, I've been given this amazing family and incredible opportunity to tell our story. I attribute this to God's grace. Like, he just decided, apart from me earning it or deserving it, to give me a story and a voice and put me in this particular moment in time to encourage people all over the world with the truth that no matter how badly you get it wrong, it's gonna be okay.

Failure isn't final.

You aren't your mistakes.

Your failures don't define you, but they can refine you.

I tend to believe that if Jesus can do something really cool with a guy who gets it wrong nonstop like me, he can do something really cool with you too!

CANCELING CANCEL CULTURE

So why don't we just dispose of the notion that broken, flawed people need to be canceled? Maybe they just need to be loved. Maybe respectfully enlightened or challenged. Maybe invited for Thanksgiving dinner or, at the very least, a coffee. Maybe they just need grace.

Perhaps *we all* just need a little more grace for ourselves and for others. Perhaps instead of tearing ourselves and one another down, we would be wise to build one another up. It's easy to criticize; it's harder to encourage. It's easy to throw stones; it's harder to build bridges. But maybe that's what we all need.

We need each other.

I need you and you need me and he needs her and she needs him and, well, you get the point.

That's not to say we shouldn't advocate for justice, even passionately so! That's why our family looks the way it looks. We saw the need, even the injustice, that there were children without forever families for reasons out of their control and knew we needed to do something about it. And we fought hard to change that reality.

When it's dark, it's a lot more productive to turn on a light than curse the fact that you can't see anything. And when something's wrong in the world, it's a lot more constructive to do something about it than to stand around complaining about it on social media.

It is possible to stand up for what is right while doing it in kindness, compassion, and empathy. And perhaps that is the best reason of all for doing the right thing.

I dare say most of us are already keenly aware of our failures and shortcomings—perhaps more sharply than anyone else on the planet. We don't necessarily need to be reminded over and over. Sometimes we just need someone to tell us it's gonna be okay. And sometimes we just need an active example of a better way.

So that's me in this little book, trying to be that sitcom dad offering up some free (or whatever you happened to pay for this book) advice to make the world (or at least your little bit of creation we call your heart) a better place.

Have a little more grace for yourself. Have a little more grace for others.

I promise you, it's gonna be okay.

AFTERWORD

BY AMANDA MILLER

Stephen and I will have been married for nineteen years by the time this book releases, and looking back, it feels like we've lived through an incredible amount of "life" in those years. From ministry and entrepreneurship to miscarriages, births, and adoptions, our lives have certainly not been dull.

Because of our presence on social media, we often hear comments regarding our family's appearance and how it looks like we're living the dream life. In one sense, I can relate to that sentiment because I look at our beautiful children and this life we're building together, and it moves me to tears. I'm so deeply grateful for it all. But it hasn't come without pain. In fact, sometimes it feels like we've endured more than our fair share of challenges and grief, many of which we've shared openly over the years. We would never want to portray our life as perfect or easy, and yet we are firm believers in spreading hope and joy to those around us. How do we do this during those really dark, sometimes heartbreaking seasons we all inevitably go through? This is a question we strive to answer well on this journey.

Through it all, we've seen God sustain us in ways only he can do, and our hope is to connect with others in a way that is encouraging and offers hope, not because we have the answers or don't make mistakes (i.e., why this book is called *The Art of Getting It Wrong*), but rather because, despite our humanity, there's always hope for the future, for growth, for healing, for redemption, and for goodness to come out of those challenging seasons.

This book was written with that truth in mind, and I've been privileged to witness my husband pour so much of his heart into these pages over the past year or so. We hope that through sharing some of our experiences, you'll be encouraged to know that failure isn't final and that there is always hope for the future, despite any current circumstances you may be walking though. You are dearly loved through it all.

Stephen, I am so incredibly proud of you for your perseverance, your charisma and joy, and your dedication to your family and your faith. I love this crazy, wild journey we're on together and feel blessed to be able to do all these things by your side.

ACKNOWLEDGMENTS

My entire life has been built on the shoulders of giants. Not literal giants, but there are a couple of pretty tall people on the list. And even though a few sentences here at the conclusion of this book can't come close to describing the gratitude I have for the people who have poured into me and my family, I want to say thank you.

Jesus—I'm humbled beyond words to be yours. Grateful beyond words for the gift of your grace in having first chosen me and called me your own. I wasn't last-picked with you; I was first-picked. You made me in your image, redeemed me by your work on the cross, adopted me into your family, and gave me everything I have.

Amanda—I really don't deserve your kindness and patience and unmatched love. Not only have you walked with me through every page of this book, but you've walked with me through a good majority of the stories in it in real time (plus a whole lot more), and I'm in awe that you still love me and haven't given up on a joker like me. You're the strongest, bravest, and most incredible woman I have ever met. I'm crazy about you, and I'm so thankful to have you as my partner in crime.

Reese, Penny, Keira, Jude, Liam, Ethan, and Lincoln (a.k.a. the Juice Box Biker Gang)—you seven are the pride of your mom's and my lives. You have walked through so much and seen more craziness in your short years than many may ever see. I'm in awe of all of you and can't think of a higher calling and honor in this life than that we get to be your parents.

Mom and Dad—I am who I am because you are who you are. Thank you both for always encouraging me in my passions and pursuits.

Charles and Sonii—thank you for making such an exquisitely perfect woman like your daughter and not picking up everything and moving to another country far, far away when I asked her to marry me. And for all the love, support, and wise counsel you have given us over the years. And I just want to reiterate—for your superhot daughter I get to call my wife. *Big* thanks on that one.

Charlie Harrisberger, Matt Carter, Tom Mosley, Jim Frith, and Darrin Patrick—you guys taught me to love Jesus, be a godly husband and dad, and own my mistakes, and in so many ways how to be a man. Thank you for your friendship and guidance over the years.

Tom Dean and Andy Rogers—thank you for believing in this book and making it a reality. We make a great team, and I can't wait to see all we get to do together over the years.

And finally, thank you so much to Charley Button and our team at Select—you're the best management team we could have ever hoped for, and we are so grateful for you!

NOTES

1. Disclaimer: this statement has not been evaluated by the FDA, FTC, YMCA, NCAA, IMDB, or any other organization with cool initials.
2. "Pennies from Heaven," track 7 on Louis Prima, *The Call of the Wildest*, Capitol Records, 1957, LP.
3. See "Directory of Mark Twain's Maxims, Quotations, and Various Opinions," Twainquotes.com, accessed October 25, 2021, www.twain quotes.com/Death.html.
4. Quoted in Lewis Howes, "20 Lessons from Walt Disney on Entrepreneurship, Innovation, and Chasing Your Dreams," *Forbes*, July 17, 2012, www.forbes.com/sites/lewishowes/2012/07/17/20-business-quotes-and-lessons-from-walt-disney.
5. Quoted in Travis Bradberry, "8 Ways Smart People Use Failure to Their Advantage," *Forbes*, April 12, 2016, www.forbes.com/sites/travisbradberry/2016/04/12/8-ways-smart-people-use-failure-to-their-advantage.
6. *Garth Brooks in . . . the Life of Chris Gaines*, Capitol Records, 1999.
7. For example, "Lost in You," track 2 on *Garth Brooks in . . . the Life of Chris Gaines*.
8. Lyndsey Parker, "Garth Brooks Opens Up about Chris Gaines Era: 'My Ribs Are Still Sore from Getting the S*** Kicked Out of Me for It,'" Yahoo, September 27, 2019, www.yahoo.com/now/garth-brooks-opens-up-about-chris-gaines-era-my-ribs-are-still-sore-from-getting-the-s-kicked-out-of-me-for-it-200451806.html.
9. Psalm 139:13–14 reads, "For you created my inmost being; you knit me together in my mother's womb. I praise you because I am fearfully and wonderfully made; your works are wonderful, I know that full well."
10. Bill Gates, *The Road Ahead*, rev. ed. (New York: Penguin, 1996), 38.

11. Ed Catmull, *Creativity, Inc.: Overcoming the Unseen Forces That Stand in the Way of True Inspiration* (New York: Random House, 2014), 109.

12. *Ted Lasso*, season 1, episode 2, "Biscuits," directed by Zach Braff, written by Jason Sudeikis, Brendan Hunt, and Joe Kelly, starring Jason Sudeikis, aired August 14, 2020, on Apple TV+.

13. "Sorry," track 4 on Justin Bieber, *Purpose*, Def Jam Recordings, 2015.

14. "Apologize," featuring OneRepublic, track 16 on Timbaland, *Shock Value*, Interscope Records, 2007.

15. From *Home Alone*, directed by Chris Columbus, written by John Hughes, starring Macaulay Culkin (Los Angeles: 20th Century Fox, 1990).

16. "The Climb," track 8 on Miley Cyrus, *Hannah Montana: The Movie*, Walt Disney Records, 2009.

17. "Seven," track 7 on Sleeping at Last, *Atlas: Enneagram*, Asteroid B-612, 2019.

18. Matthew 6:34.

19. *A League of Their Own*, directed by Penny Marshall, screenplay by Lowell Ganz and Babaloo Mandel, story by Kim Wilson and Kelly Candaele, starring Tom Hanks and Geena Davis (Columbia Pictures, 1992).

20. *Braveheart*, directed by Mel Gibson, written by Randall Wallace, starring Mel Gibson (Hollywood: Paramount Pictures, 1995).

21. *Billy Madison*, directed by Tamra Davis, written by Tim Herlihy and Adam Sandler, starring Adam Sandler (Hollywood: Universal Pictures, 1995).

22. *Ferris Bueller's Day Off*, written and directed by John Hughes, starring Matthew Broderick (Hollywood: Paramount Pictures, 1986).

23. Lamentations 3:22–23 ESV.

24. Gene Wilder, vocalist, "Pure Imagination," by Leslie Bricusse and Anthony Newley, performed in *Willy Wonka & the Chocolate Factory* (Hollywood: Paramount Pictures, 1971).

25. *Fight Club*, directed by David Fincher, starring Brad Pitt and Edward Norton (Los Angeles: 20th Century Fox, 1999).

26. "The Times They Are A-Changin'," track 1 on Bob Dylan, *The Times They Are A-Changin'*, Columbia Records, 1964.

27. Wikipedia contributors, "Princess Peach," *Wikipedia*, https://en.wikipedia.org/wiki/Princess_Peach.

28. See John 8:32; 14:6; 16:13; 17:17.

29. *Ted Lasso*, season 2, episode 7, "Headspace," directed by Matt Lipsy, written by Phoebe Wilson, starring Jason Sudeikis, aired September 3, 2021, on Apple TV+.

30. Stephen Miller, *Worship Leaders, We Are Not Rock Stars* (Chicago: Moody, 2013).

31. "Thankfulness Song," track 7 on *VeggieTales Sing-Alongs: Junior's Bedtime Songs*, Big Idea, 2002.

SHARE YOUR STORY OF GETTING IT WRONG!

When was the last time you totally got it wrong?

What was your last epic fail?

When was the last time you thought everything was going to fall apart, but it was all okay in the end?

Share your story with me! Post your story on social media with #theartofgettingitwrong and tag me! @themillerfam and @stephenmiller

FOLLOW THE MILLER FAM ONLINE

- Facebook - themillerfam
- Instagram - @themillerfam
- YouTube - graceforthemillers
- TikTok - @themillerfam
- Website - www.themillerfam.co

STEPHEN MILLER MUSIC

- Website: stephen-miller.com
- Facebook - @StephenMillerMusic
- Twitter - @StephenMiller
- Instagram - @stephenmiller
- YouTube.com/stephenmillermusic

FIND MY MUSIC ON